Workbook

Science

Editorial Offices: Glenview, Illinois • Parsippany, New Jersey • New York, New York
Sales Offices: Needham, Massachusetts • Duluth, Georgia • Glenview, Illinois
Coppell, Texas • Sacramento, California • Mesa, Arizona

www.sfsuccessnet.com

PEARSON

Scott
Foresman

Series Authors

Dr. Timothy Cooney

Professor of Earth Science and Science Education
University of Northern Iowa (UNI)
Cedar Falls, Iowa

Dr. Jim Cummins

Professor
Department of Curriculum,
Teaching, and Learning
The University of Toronto
Toronto, Canada

Dr. James Flood

Distinguished Professor of Literacy and Language
School of Teacher Education
San Diego State University
San Diego, California

Barbara Kay Foots, M.Ed.

Science Education Consultant
Houston, Texas

Dr. M. Jenice Goldston

Associate Professor of Science Education
Department of Elementary Education Programs
University of Alabama
Tuscaloosa, Alabama

Dr. Shirley Gholston Key

Associate Professor of Science Education
Instruction and Curriculum Leadership Department
College of Education
University of Memphis
Memphis, Tennessee

Dr. Diane Lapp

Distinguished Professor of Reading and Language Arts in Teacher Education
San Diego State University
San Diego, California

Sheryl A. Mercier

Classroom Teacher
Dunlap Elementary School
Dunlap, California

Dr. Karen L. Ostlund

UTeach, College of Natural Sciences
The University of Texas at Austin
Austin, Texas

Dr. Nancy Romance

Professor of Science Education & Principal Investigator
NSF/IERI Science IDEAS Project
Charles E. Schmidt College of Science
Florida Atlantic University
Boca Raton, Florida

Dr. William Tate

Chair and Professor of Education and Applied Statistics
Department of Education
Washington University
St. Louis, Missouri

Dr. Kathryn C. Thornton

Professor
School of Engineering and Applied Science
University of Virginia
Charlottesville, Virginia

Dr. Leon Ukens

Professor of Science Education
Department of Physics, Astronomy, and Geosciences
Towson University
Towson, Maryland

Steve Weinberg

Consultant
Connecticut Center for Advanced Technology
East Hartford, Connecticut

Consulting Author

Dr. Michael P. Klentschy

Superintendent
El Centro Elementary School District
El Centro, California

ISBN: 0-328-12614-4

ISBN: 0-328-20068-9

9 10 V084 13 12 11 10 09 08 07 06

© Pearson Education, Inc.

Unit A
Life Science

Unit B
Earth Science

Name __Tyler wilson__

Circle the letter of your answer.

1. The word **classify** means to put things, such as plants and animals, into groups. Which characteristic would **not** be used to classify animals?

   A. leaf size
   B. types of organs
   C. food
   D. life cycle

2. A **vertebrate** is an animal that has a spine, or backbone. Which animal is a vertebrate?

   A. starfish
   B. bee
   C. tiger
   D. lobster

3. An **invertebrate** is an animal that has no spine, or backbone. Which animal is an invertebrate?

   A. cheetah
   B. monkey
   C. jellyfish
   D. dog

Scientists use a special system to put living things into groups. Use the code below to find out some of the names of these groups. Write the letters in the blanks.

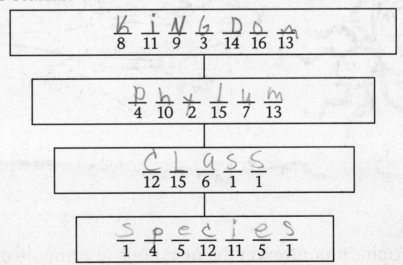

K I N G D O M
8 11 9 3 14 16 13

P H Y L U M
4 10 2 15 7 13

C L A S S
12 15 6 1 1

S P E C I E S
1 4 5 12 11 5 1

1 = S	5 = E	9 = N	13 = M
2 = Y	6 = A	10 = H	14 = D
3 = G	7 = U	11 = I	15 = L
4 = P	8 = K	12 = C	16 = O

Notes for Home: Your child learned the vocabulary terms for Chapter 1.
Home Activity: Place the *kingdom, phylum, class,* and *species* cards in the hierarchy shown and discuss their relationship to one another. Then name some animals and have your child *classify* each as a *vertebrate* or an *invertebrate*.

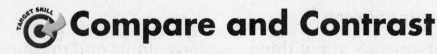
Compare and Contrast

Read the science article.

Spiders and Lizards

Spiders and lizards are both members of the animal kingdom. Both are cold-blooded animals. Their body temperature changes with their environment. Spiders are members of the arachnid class of invertebrates. Invertebrates are animals without backbones. Lizards belong to the reptile class of vertebrates. Vertebrates are animals with backbones. Spiders have eight legs, and most lizards have four legs. A few lizards are legless. Spiders and most lizards lay eggs. Insects make up a spider's diet and are a part of the diet of most lizards too. Most lizards also eat small animals, but some eat plants.

Apply It!

Use the graphic organizer on the next page to compare and contrast spiders and lizards.

© Pearson Education, Inc.

Name _____

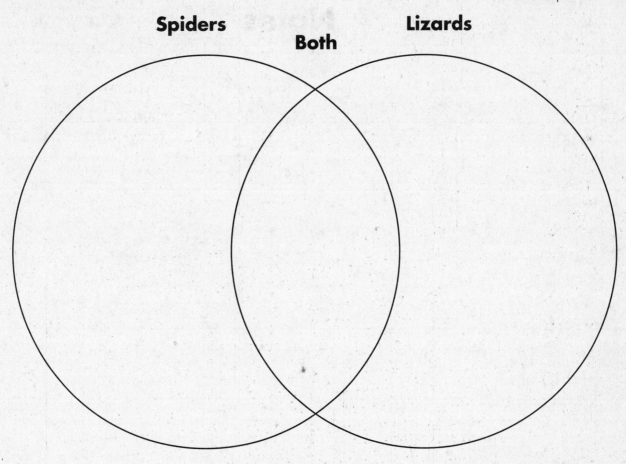

Spiders   **Both**   **Lizards**

Notes for Home: Your child learned how to compare and contrast two organisms.
Home Activity: Have your child use a chart to compare and contrast two common objects found in your home, such as a refrigerator and a stove or a vacuum cleaner and a broom.

Notes

Lesson 1: Why do we classify?

Before You Read Lesson 1

Read each statement below. Place a check mark in the circle to indicate whether you agree or disagree with the statement.

	Agree	Disagree
1. Scientists use a classification system to categorize plants and animals.	○	○
2. Scientists classify plants and animals using certain characteristics.	○	○
3. Phylum is the name of the first level in the classification system.	○	○
4. There are more organisms in the genus level than at the order level.	○	○

After You Read Lesson 1

Reread each statement above. If the lesson supports your choice, place a check mark in the *Correct* circle. Then explain how the text supports your choice. If the lesson does not support your choice, place a check mark in the *Incorrect* circle. Then explain why your choice is wrong.

	Correct	Incorrect
1. _____ _____	○	○
2. _____ _____	○	○
3. _____ _____	○	○
4. _____ _____	○	○

 Notes for Home: Your child has completed a pre/post inventory of key concepts in the lesson.
Home Activity: Help your child create a mnemonic, or memory device, to help him or her remember the names of the seven classification levels.

Reviewing Terms: Matching

Match each definition with the correct word. Write the letter on the line next to the definition.

_A_ 1. the highest and most general group of organisms

_C_ 2. the level of classification below phylum

_b_ 3. to put things into groups

_E_ 4. the next level of classification below the level of kingdom

_d_ 5. the level of classification with the least variety of organisms

a. kingdom
b. classify
c. class
d. species
e. phylum

Reviewing Concepts: True or False

Write **T** (True) or **F** (False) on the line before each statement.

True 6. A classification system makes it easier for scientists to communicate about specific organisms.

True 7. Today's classification system is still changing.

False 8. Archaebacteria and Eubacteria belong to the same kingdom.

Applying Strategies: Draw Conclusions

Use complete sentences to answer question 9. (2 points)

9. Why is there more variety in a kingdom than there is in a species? Give an example.

_____

_____

_____

_____

Lesson 2: How do we classify vertebrates?

Before You Read Lesson 2

Read each statement below. Place a check mark in the circle to indicate whether you agree or disagree with the statement.

	Agree	Disagree
1. Animals with a backbone are called invertebrates.	○	○
2. Mammals, reptiles, birds, amphibians, and fish are all vertebrates.	○	○
3. Reptiles and birds have similar life cycles.	○	○
4. The body temperature of cold-blooded animals does not change.	○	○

After You Read Lesson 2

Reread each statement above. If the lesson supports your choice, place a check mark in the *Correct* circle. Then explain how the text supports your choice. If the lesson does not support your choice, place a check mark in the *Incorrect* circle. Then explain why your choice is wrong.

	Correct	Incorrect
1. _____	○	○
_____		
2. _____	○	○
_____		
3. _____	○	○
_____		
4. _____	○	○
_____		

Notes for Home: Your child has completed a pre/post inventory of key concepts in the lesson.
Home Activity: Have your child explain the similarities and differences between mammals and fish. Put the information on a Venn diagram.

Reviewing Terms: Matching

Match each definition or example with the correct term. Write the letter of the term on the line next to the definition or example.

___mammals___ 1. animals that make milk for their young

___vertebrates___ 2. organisms with backbones

___reptiles___ 3. cold-blooded animals with tough, dry skin with scales

___birds___ 4. animals with feathers

___amphibians___ 5. animals with skin that can absorb water and oxygen

___fish___ 6. the class of vertebrates with only water-living animals

_____ a. fish
_____ b. birds
_____ c. reptiles
_____ d. vertebrates
_____ e. mammals
_____ f. amphibians

Reviewing Main Ideas: Sentence Completion

Complete the sentence with the correct word or phrase.

___changes___ 7. The body temperature of a cold-blooded animal _____ as the temperature of the air or water around it changes. (changes, remains the same)

___hair___ 8. Mammals differ from reptiles because mammals have _____ covering their bodies. (hair, scales)

Writing

Use complete sentences to answer question 9. (2 points)

9. Describe how today's lizards are thought to be like and different from many dinosaurs.

_____

_____

_____

_____

_____

Name __Tyler wilson__

Lesson 3: How do we classify invertebrates?

Before You Read Lesson 3

Read each statement below. Place a check mark in the circle to indicate whether you agree or disagree with the statement.

	Agree	Disagree
1. There are more vertebrates than invertebrates living on Earth.	✓	○
2. Mollusks are not invertebrates because some have an outer shell.	✓	○
3. Arthropods make up the largest animal phylum.	○	○
4. Lobsters, spiders, and houseflies are all arthropods.	○	✓

After You Read Lesson 3

Reread each statement above. If the lesson supports your choice, place a check mark in the *Correct* circle. Then explain how the text supports your choice. If the lesson does not support your choice, place a check mark in the *Incorrect* circle. Then explain why your choice is wrong.

	Correct	Incorrect
1. According to the passage my anseru is right because it sayt in the book	✓	○
2. _____	○	○
3. _____	○	○
4. _____	○	○

Notes for Home: Your child has completed a pre/post inventory of key concepts in the lesson.
Home Activity: With your child, make a collage of different types of invertebrates. Draw pictures or use pictures from newspapers and magazines.

Reviewing Terms: Sentence Completion

Complete each sentence with the correct term.

vertebrates   invertebrates

vertebrates 1. Most animals on Earth are _____.

vertebrates 2. Animals with backbones are called _____.

invertebrates 3. Mollusks with a hard outer shell are _____.

Reviewing Concepts: True or False

Write **T** (True) or **F** (False) on the line before each statement.

false 4. Some arthropods are vertebrates.

True 5. Jellyfish and coral belong to the same phylum Cnidaria.

false 6. A chrysalis appears during the first stage of complete metamorphosis.

True 7. A dichotomous key is used to identify an unknown organism.

True 8. Earthworms are segmented worms.

Writing

Use complete sentences to answer question 9. (2 points)

9. How are complete metamorphosis and incomplete metamorphosis in insects alike and different?

_____

_____

_____

_____

_____

Lesson 4: How are other organisms classified?

Before You Read Lesson 4

Read each statement below. Place a check mark in the circle to indicate whether you agree or disagree with the statement.

	Agree	Disagree
1. Plants are multicellular organisms.	○	○
2. *Vascular* means that nutrients are carried throughout a plant by special tubes.	○	○
3. Conifers are different from ferns in that conifers do not have leaves.	○	○
4. All organisms are classified either as plants or as animals.	○	○

After You Read Lesson 4

Reread each statement above. If the lesson supports your choice, place a check mark in the *Correct* circle. Then explain how the text supports your choice. If the lesson does not support your choice, place a check mark in the *Incorrect* circle. Then explain why your choice is wrong.

	Correct	Incorrect
1. _____	○	○
_____		
2. _____	○	○
_____		
3. _____	○	○
_____		
4. _____	○	○
_____		

Notes for Home: Your child has completed a pre/post inventory of key concepts in the lesson.
Home Activity: Take a walk with your child. Find and list examples of plant organisms.

Reviewing Main Ideas: Sentence Completion

Complete each sentence with the correct term.

_____ 1. Plants use sunlight, water, and _____ to make food. (carbon dioxide, oxygen)

_____ 2. Members of the plant kingdom are _____. (single-celled, multicellular)

_____ 3. Ferns and mosses reproduce by _____. (seeds, spores)

_____ 4. Mosses are _____ plants. (vascular, nonvascular)

_____ 5. Conifers _____ leaves. (have, do not have)

_____ 6. Flowering plants use their flowers to make _____ for reproduction. (seeds, conifers)

_____ 7. Fungi _____ plants because they cannot make their own sugar for food. (are, are not)

_____ 8. One popular classification system uses _____ kingdoms. (five, six)

Applying Strategies: Find a Percentage

9. A garden contains 20 different species of plants. Five of these plants are ferns. What percent of the garden is made up of ferns? Show your work. (2 points)

Classifying Triangles

When polygons are classified by number of sides, the three-sided polygons are called triangles. Triangles may be classified by their angles or the relative lengths of their sides.

Classification by angles:

An **acute triangle** has only acute angles.

A **right triangle** has exactly one right angle and two acute angles.

An **obtuse triangle** has exactly one obtuse angle and two acute angles.

A  B  C

Use the triangles above to help you complete each sentence.

1. Triangle A is a(n) _____ triangle.

2. Triangle B is a(n) _____ triangle.

3. Triangle C is a(n) _____ triangle.

Classification by sides:

A **scalene triangle** has three sides of different lengths.

An **isosceles triangle** has at least two sides of equal length.

An **equilateral triangle** has all three sides of equal length.

D  E F

Use the triangles above to help you complete each sentence.

4. The isosceles triangle that is not also equilateral is triangle _____.

5. The scalene triangle is triangle _____.

6. The equilateral triangle is triangle _____.

 Notes for Home: Your child learned how to classify geometric figures according to specific characteristics.
Home Activity: Help your child look for triangles in everyday objects. Together classify the triangles by their sides and by their angles.

Notes

Dear Family,

Your child is learning about how living things are classified. In the science chapter Classifying Organisms, our class has learned how the six kingdoms of living things are named and grouped. The children have also learned to look for similarities and differences between living things that will help them compare, contrast, and classify all kinds of organisms.

In addition to learning how to classify different kinds of living things, the children have also learned many new vocabulary words. Help your child to make these words a part of his or her own vocabulary by using them when you talk together about living things.

classify
kingdom
phylum
class
species
vertebrate
invertebrate

The following pages include activities that you and your child can do together. By participating in your child's education, you will help to bring the learning home.

Family Science Activity

Exploring Natural Diversity

Take a family nature walk to discover and classify the variety of living things around you. You don't need to go far—there are hundreds of living things in your neighborhood alone.

Living Thing	Appearance	Classification
Spider	Small, eight legs	Invertebrate

1. Prepare the chart before you leave. Bring pens or pencils for each person.

2. When you find a living thing, write it down in the chart. You can write a description even if you do not know the name for a plant or animal you find.

3. Begin to make some classifications during your walk. For example, write if an organism is a plant or animal or if it is a vertebrate or invertebrate.

4. Review the things you classified when you get home. You might be able to make more detailed classifications using an encyclopedia or the Internet.

5. Ask questions to review and expand your journey:
   • Did we find more vertebrates or invertebrates?
   • How many mammals did we see?
   • Where could we go next time to see more amphibians?
   • Where might we find more fungi?

Workbook

Vocabulary Practice

Use the clues to write each of the vocabulary words in the crossword puzzle below.

Classifying Living Things

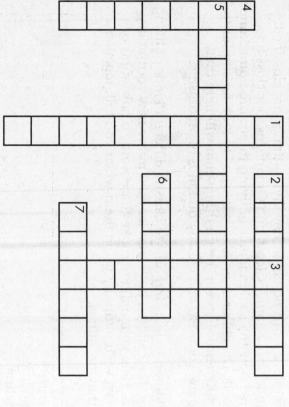

Across

2 the smallest level of classification
5 without a backbone
6 the level of classification below phylum
7 the second level of classification

Down

1 with a backbone
3 to put into groups
4 the largest level of classification

Classifying Animals

One way to classify an animal depends on whether or not it has a backbone. A vertebrate has a backbone. An invertebrate has no backbone.

Classify each animal on the list as a vertebrate or invertebrate.

Animal	Vertebrate or Invertebrate?
Rattlesnake	
Butterfly	
Crab	
Eagle	
Earthworm	
Shark	
Clam	
Hamster	

Circle the vocabulary word in the parentheses that you think makes each sentence correct. After you read Chapter 2, review your answers.

1. The (cell membrane, nucleus, vacuole) allows nutrients to enter the cell.

2. All the parts of the cell outside of the nucleus are found in the gooey fluid of the (vacuole, chloroplast, cytoplasm).

3. The (cytoplasm, nucleus, organ) is the control center of the cell.

4. Storing nutrients and breaking down wastes is the job of the (tissue, cell membrane, vacuole) of a cell.

5. The (cytoplasts, chloroplasts, organs) of plant cells produce oxygen and sugar from water and carbon dioxide.

6. The stomach, mouth, and intestines are all part of a(n) (organ system, organ, tissue).

7. The (cell wall, cell membrane, cytoplasm) is a stiff outer covering that protects plant cells.

8. Groups of tissues that perform certain jobs in your body are called (vacuoles, organs, mitochondria).

9. Groups of bone cells in your body make up bone (chloroplasts, cytoplasts, tissue).

© Pearson Education, Inc.

Notes for Home: Your child learned the vocabulary terms for Chapter 2.
Home Activity: Have your child write each vocabulary word on one side of an index card and write the word's definition on the other side. Use the cards to quiz your child.

Draw Conclusions

Read the science article.

Needs of Plants

Plants need sunlight, soil, air, and water to live. In a recent science experiment, two plants were given the same amounts of sunlight, soil, and air. Plant A was given the amount of water that a plant needs to survive, while Plant B was not given any water.

Apply It!

What conclusion can you draw about the future of the two plants? Use the graphic organizer on the next page to write your facts and your conclusion.

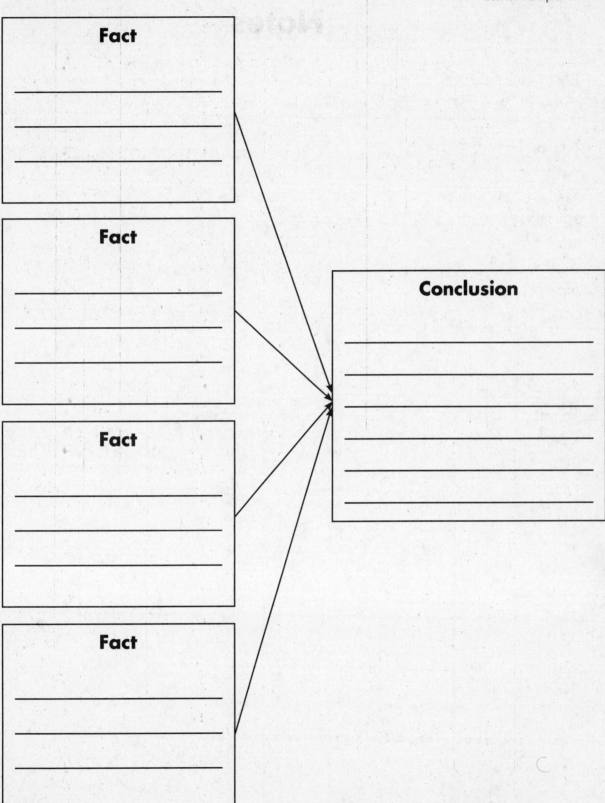

Fact

_____

_____

_____

Fact

_____

_____

_____

Fact

_____

_____

_____

Fact

_____

_____

_____

Conclusion

_____

_____

_____

_____

_____

_____

_____

Notes for Home: Your child learned how to draw conclusions based on facts.
Home Activity: Look at a recipe for a favorite food. Ask your child what might happen to the food if you do not add all the ingredients or the correct amounts of the ingredients.

Notes

Name _____

Lesson 2: How do cells work together?

Before You Read Lesson 2

Read each statement below. Place a check mark in the circle to indicate whether you agree or disagree with the statement.

	Agree	Disagree
1. All cells have the same shape and size.	○	○
2. Tissue is made up of similar types of cells that carry out the same functions.	○	○
3. The largest human organ is the brain.	○	○
4. The cells that make up your skin form many layers.	○	○

After You Read Lesson 2

Reread each statement above. If the lesson supports your choice, place a check mark in the *Correct* circle. Then explain how the text supports your choice. If the lesson does not support your choice, place a check mark in the *Incorrect* circle. Then explain why your choice is wrong.

	Correct	Incorrect
1. _____ _____	○	○
2. _____ _____	○	○
3. _____ _____	○	○
4. _____ _____	○	○

Notes for Home: Your child has completed a pre/post inventory of key concepts in the lesson.
Home Activity: Ask your child to explain the differences between branching cells, round cells, and flat cells. Have your child draw a picture of each type of cell.

Reviewing Terms: Matching

Match each definition with the correct term. Write the letter on the line next to the definition or example of the term.

__b__ 1. a group of the same kind of cells working together doing the same job

__b__ 2. a flower

__b__ 3. bone cells

__A__ 4. a grouping of different tissues combined together into one structure

a. organ
b. tissue

Reviewing Concepts: True or False

Write **T** (True) or **F** (False) on the line before each statement.

__F__ 5. Sweat evaporates, keeping the body warm.

__F__ 6. The outer layer of the skin is made up of living cells.

__T__ 7. Red blood cells carry oxygen to all your cells.

__F__ 8. Nerve tissues help keep skin soft.

Writing

Use complete sentences to answer question 9. (2 points)

9. What evidence is there that skin is an organ?

_____

_____

_____

_____

Lesson 3: How do organs work together?

Before You Read Lesson 3

Read each statement below. Place a check mark in the circle to indicate whether you agree or disagree with the statement.

	Agree	Disagree
1. An organ system is made up of organs and tissues that perform a special job.	○	○
2. You can control the movement of about 640 muscles in your body.	○	○
3. Your skeletal system is not considered an organ system.	○	○
4. All your body's muscles are connected to bones.	○	○

After You Read Lesson 3

Reread each statement above. If the lesson supports your choice, place a check mark in the *Correct* circle. Then explain how the text supports your choice. If the lesson does not support your choice, place a check mark in the *Incorrect* circle. Then explain why your choice is wrong.

	Correct	Incorrect
1. _____	○	○
_____		
2. _____	○	○
_____		
3. _____	○	○
_____		
4. _____	○	○
_____		

Notes for Home child has completed a pre/post inventory of key concepts in the lesson.
Home Activity place with your child. Ask your child to explain how the body's muscle   nd nerves work together to make these movements.

Reviewing Terms: Sentence Completion

Complete each sentence with the correct word or phrase.

organ system 1. The skeletal system is an example of an _____. (organ, organ system)

muscle 2. You have about 640 _____ that you can control. (muscles, organs)

Reviewing Main Ideas: True or False

Write **T** (True) or **F** (False) on the line before each statement.

_F_ 3. Organ systems do not interact with one another.

_T_ 4. About 100 bones make up the skeletal system.

_F_ 5. When you shiver, muscles are contracting to warm your body.

_T_ 6. Muscles only push bones to make them move.

_T_ 7. One job of the skeletal system is to protect important organs.

_T_ 8. The nervous system controls how your muscles move your bones.

Applying Strategies: Calculate

Use the following information to answer question 9. (2 points)

9. In one year, doctors at the emergency room of a hospital treated 380 children for bicycle accidents. Of these, 15 percent had a broken collarbone. How many children were treated for a broken collarbone? Show your work.

the anserw is 395

Very Large Numbers in Astronomy

Very large numbers are needed to express many measurements in astronomy. Numbers used in astronomy extend beyond trillions to include quadrillions (a quadrillion is a 1 followed by 15 zeros) and quintillions (a 1 followed by 18 zeros). For example, the planet Mercury weighs about 364 quintillion (364,000,000,000,000,000,000) tons.

Write each underlined number in standard form on the line.

1. Mercury's average distance from the Sun is about <u>36 million</u> miles.

   _____

2. Our own planet Earth averages a distance of <u>93 million</u> miles from the Sun.

   _____

3. At a speed of about <u>186 thousand</u> miles per second, light from the Sun takes about 8 minutes to reach Earth.

   _____

4. The Moon, Earth's only natural satellite, weighs in at a hefty <u>81 quintillion</u> tons.

   _____

5. Mars averages a distance of more than <u>141 million</u> miles from the Sun.

   _____

6. Venus is about <u>67 million, 2 hundred thousand</u> miles from the Sun.

   _____

7. Jupiter, the largest planet in our solar system, averages a distance of <u>484 million</u> miles from the Sun.

   _____

8. Pluto is the planet farthest from the Sun. It is a staggering <u>3 billion, 647 million</u> miles from its very dim and distant Sun.

   _____

Notes for Home: Your child learned how to write large numbers in standard form.
Home Activity: Together look in newspapers and magazines for large numbers, such as populations of cities and budgets of states and countries. Ask your child to read each number and write it in both words and standard form.

Notes

Dear Family,

Your child is learning about the structure of living things, beginning with cells. In the science chapter Cells to Systems, our class has learned how cells work together to form tissues, and how tissues work together to form organs. The children are investigating the building blocks from which living things form their wonderful complexity and variety.

In addition to learning how plant and animal cells are similar and different, the children have also learned many new vocabulary words that are used to describe the structures of organisms. Help your child to make these words a part of his or her own vocabulary by using them when you talk together about living things.

cell membrane
vacuole
nucleus
cytoplasm
cell wall
chloroplast
tissue
organ
organ system

The following pages include activities that you and your child can do together. By participating in your child's education, you will help to bring the learning home.

Family Science Activity

Making Cell Models

When we study cells, we often look at photographs or diagrams. As a result, students often think that cells are flat. You can help your child remember that cells are actually three-dimensional by working together to create colorful models of red blood cells.

Materials
- modeling clay
- cardboard

Steps

❶ Take a lump of modeling clay and shape it like a rounded disc.

❷ Make a large dimple in the center of the disc.

❸ Mount the disc on the cardboard.

❹ Continue to make more discs until you have a cluster of them on the cardboard.

❺ Label the cluster of discs "Red Blood Cells."

Talk About It

Where in your body are red blood cells made?
What do red blood cells do?
How do the shapes of red blood cells help them do their work?

Vocabulary Practice

Structures of Living Things

Write the vocabulary words that answer each clue.
Then use the numbered letters to answer the riddle.

1. where chromosomes are in a cell

n u c l e u s
             13

2. a group of tissues combined together into one
structure

o r g a n
       4

3. the contents of a cell outside the nucleus

c y t o p l a s m
       8   2

4. these act like stomachs in a cell

v a c u o l e s
  12

5. it surrounds every cell

c e l l
     10
m e m b r a n e
     3

6. they give plants their green color

c h l o r o p l a s t s
          11   9

7. a group of organs and tissues working
together

o r g a n s y s t e m
                          5

8. a group of the same kind of cells working
together doing the same job

t i s s u e
7

9. the tough material that surrounds plant cells

c e l l   w a l l
      1   9

The skin is the l a r g e s t organ
               1 2 3 4 5 6 7

in the human body. By weight, it makes up about

t w e l v e percent of the body.
8 9 10 11 12 13

Fun Fact

Scientists estimate that there are between 10 and
100 trillion cells in the human body. One trillion
is 1,000,000,000,000, or a million millions.

Answers: 1. nucleus, 2. organ, 3. cytoplasm, 4. vacuoles, 5. cell membrane, 6. chloroplasts,
7. organ system, 8. tissue, 9. cell wall; largest, twelve

Name _Tyler wilson_

Vocabulary Preview

Use with Chapter 3.

Predict what you think each vocabulary word means. After you finish reading Chapter 3, change or add to your definitions. Then draw a simple sketch to go with each word.

Vocabulary	Predict the Meaning	Draw a Simple Sketch
vein	are blood vessels that take blood to and from your heart	
artery	are blood vesels the carry blood away from your heart	
valve	are flaps that act like doors to keep blood flowing	
capillary	are small kinds of blood vessels	
mucus	is a sticky, thick fluid that traps dust, germs, and other things in the air.	
trachea	is a tube that carries air from the larxnx to the lungs	
bronchioles	branch into smaller and smaller part	
air sacs	are where oxygen enters the blood	
esophagus		

Notes for Home: Your child learned the vocabulary terms for Chapter 3.
Home Activity: Have your child briefly describe the purposes of the circulatory, respiratory, and digestive systems and explain how these systems work together.

Workbook

Vocabulary Preview **21**

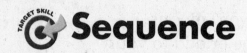

Sequence

Read the paragraph.

Process of Hearing

The process of hearing involves several steps. First, sound in the form of waves enters the outer ear and travels through the ear canal. Eventually, the sound waves hit the ear drum, causing it to vibrate. Next, these vibrations move tiny bones in the middle ear. Then the vibrations travel into the inner ear where there are nerve cells. Finally, the tiny hairs on the cells pick up the vibrations and send messages, through nerves, to the brain.

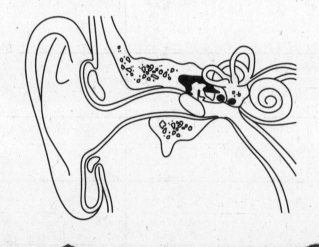

Apply It!

Write the sequence of steps from the article in the boxes in the graphic organizer on page 23.

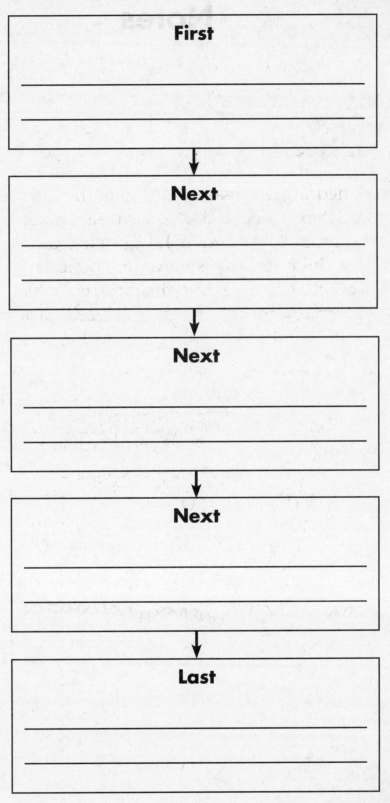

First

_____

_____

↓

Next

_____

_____

↓

Next

_____

_____

↓

Next

_____

_____

↓

Last

_____

_____

© Pearson Education, Inc.

Notes for Home: Your child learned how to put scientific information into sequential order.
Home Activity: Have your child sequence the events of his or her school day. Then discuss the events of your day in sequential order.

Notes

Lesson 1: What is the circulatory system?

Before You Read Lesson 1

Read each statement below. Place a check mark in the circle to indicate whether you agree or disagree with the statement.

	Agree	Disagree
1. Plasma makes up the largest part of your blood.	O	O
2. Your body is protected from disease by red blood cells.	O	O
3. Arteries carry blood to your heart.	O	O
4. Each side of your heart contains an atrium and a ventricle.	O	O

After You Read Lesson 1

Reread each statement above. If the lesson supports your choice, place a check mark in the *Correct* circle. Then explain how the text supports your choice. If the lesson does not support your choice, place a check mark in the *Incorrect* circle. Then explain why your choice is wrong.

	Correct	Incorrect
1. _____	O	O
_____		
2. _____	O	O
_____		
3. _____	O	O
_____		
4. _____	O	O
_____		

Notes for Home: Your child has completed a pre/post inventory of key concepts in the lesson.
Home Activity: Help your child list ways to promote good circulatory health. Ask your child how he or she could persuade others to practice these health tips.

Reviewing Terms: Matching

Match each description with the correct term. Write the letter of the term on the line next to the description.

_____ 1. smallest kind of blood vessel

_____ 2. flaps that act like doors to keep blood flowing in one direction

_____ 3. blood vessels that take blood from cells back to the heart

_____ 4. vessels that carry blood away from your heart to other parts of your body

a. arteries

b. capillary

c. valves

d. veins

Reviewing Concepts: True or False

Write **T** (True) or **F** (False) on the line before each statement.

_____ 5. Three types of blood cells are red blood cells, white blood cells, and blue blood cells.

_____ 6. Plasma carries food from the digestive system to your body cells.

_____ 7. Red blood cells carry oxygen to the rest of the body.

_____ 8. Platelets form a sticky clot when a blood vessel is cut.

Writing

9. Describe the path blood takes through the parts of the heart from where it enters the right atrium to when it enters the left atrium. (2 points)

_____

_____

_____

_____

_____

Lesson 2: What is the respiratory system?

Before You Read Lesson 2

Read each statement below. Place a check mark in the circle to indicate whether you agree or disagree with the statement.

	Agree	Disagree
1. Your diaphragm relaxes and moves up when you inhale.	O	O
2. Mucus helps prevent dust and dirt from entering your lungs.	O	O
3. Carbon dioxide enters the bloodstream through the air sacs.	O	O
4. The common cold is a disease of the respiratory system.	O	O

After You Read Lesson 2

Reread each statement above. If the lesson supports your choice, place a check mark in the *Correct* circle. Then explain how the text supports your choice. If the lesson does not support your choice, place a check mark in the *Incorrect* circle. Then explain why your choice is wrong.

	Correct	Incorrect
1. _____	O	O
2. _____	O	O
_____		
3. _____	O	O
_____		
4. _____	O	O
_____		

Notes for Home: Your child has completed a pre/post inventory of key concepts in the lesson.
Home Activity: Ask your child to describe what happens when you inhale and exhale and to explain how the body receives oxygen and discards carbon dioxide.

Name _____

Reviewing Terms: Matching

Match each definition with the correct term. Write the letter of the term on the line next to the definition.

_____ 1. small tubes in the lungs.

_____ 2. a sticky, thick fluid that traps dust, germs, and other things that may be in the air

_____ 3. a tube that carries air from the larynx to the lungs

_____ 4. tiny thin-walled pouches in the lungs

a. air sacs

b. bronchioles

c. mucus

d. trachea

Reviewing Concepts: Sentence Completion

Complete each sentence with the correct word or phrase.

_____ 5. When you _____, your diaphragm contracts and moves down. (inhale, exhale)

_____ 6. The tiny, hairlike structures on cells in linings of many parts of the respiratory system are called _____. (air sacs, cilia)

_____ 7. All multicellular organisms need _____ for their cells to get the energy they need. (oxygen, carbon dioxide)

_____ 8. When carbon dioxide builds up in your blood, your _____ senses this and sends a message to your diaphragm and rib muscles telling them to breathe. (brain, trachea)

Applying Strategies: Calculate

9. While sitting at your desk, you inhale an average of 19 times per minute. How many times will you inhale in 5 minutes? Show your work. (2 points)

Lesson 3: What are the digestive and urinary systems?

Before You Read Lesson 3

Read each statement below. Place a check mark in the circle to indicate whether you agree or disagree with the statement.

	Agree	Disagree
1. The digestive system helps your body break down food.	○	○
2. The esophagus uses muscles to move food to your stomach.	○	○
3. Digested food enters your bloodstream after it moves through the large intestine.	○	○

After You Read Lesson 3

Reread each statement above. If the lesson supports your choice, place a check mark in the *Correct* circle. Then explain how the text supports your choice. If the lesson does not support your choice, place a check mark in the *Incorrect* circle. Then explain why your choice is wrong.

	Correct	Incorrect
1. _____ _____	○	○
2. _____ _____	○	○
3. _____ _____	○	○

Notes for Home: Your child has completed a pre/post inventory of key concepts in the lesson.
Home Activity: Have your child use household objects to make a model of either the digestive system or the urinary system to demonstrate the system's actions.

Name _____

Reviewing Terms: Matching

Match each description with the correct term. Write the term on the line next to the description.

esophagus   kidneys   villi   saliva

_____ 1. liquid in the mouth that has chemicals that digest food

_____ 2. a tube that carries food to the stomach

_____ 3. tiny finger-shaped structures that give the small intestine more surface area to absorb food

_____ 4. a pair of organs that remove waste from your blood

Reviewing Concepts: True or False

Write **T** (True) or **F** (False) on the line before each statement.

_____ 5. Chewing is the first step of digestion.

_____ 6. When digestion is finished, the particles of digested food move into blood vessels in the small intestine.

_____ 7. Helpful bacteria live in the large intestine.

_____ 8. Water and salts are taken from wastes in the stomach.

Applying Strategies: Summarize

Use complete sentences to answer question 9. (2 points)

9. Describe how the body gets rid of cell wastes.

_____

_____

_____

_____

Average Rates of Respiration

Just as the heart keeps beating throughout your entire life, the lungs keep inflating and deflating as part of the process of providing oxygen to the blood. The rate, in breaths per minute, of this inflation/deflation is called the rate of respiration. The average at-rest rates of respiration of humans and a number of animals are given in the graph below. Use the graph to answer the questions. Circle the letter of the answer.

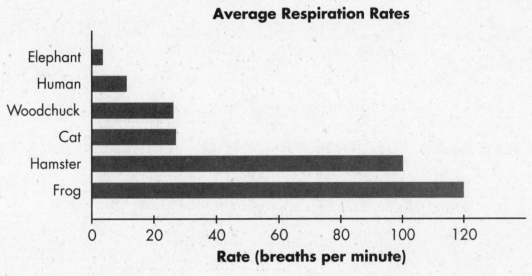

Average Respiration Rates

Rate (breaths per minute)

1. What is the best estimate of the average respiration rate of an elephant?
   A. 5 breaths per minute
   B. 10 breaths per minute
   C. 20 breaths per minute
   D. 50 breaths per minute

2. What animal has the fastest respiration rate?
   A. elephant
   B. cat
   C. hamster
   D. frog

3. What general statement can be made from the information in this graph?
   A. The larger the animal, the faster the rate of respiration.
   B. The larger the animal, the slower the rate of respiration.
   C. Animal size and rate of respiration are not related.
   D. The size of an animal depends on its rate of respiration.

Notes for Home: Your child learned how to read a bar graph and draw conclusions from data.
Home Activity: Help your child use encyclopedias or the Internet to find the maximum speeds of several animals. Ask your child to draw conclusions about animal size and top speed.

Notes

Dear Family,

Your child is learning about the human body systems and how they work together. In the science chapter Human Body Systems, the class learned about the circulatory and respiratory systems. The children also learned about the digestive and urinary systems.

In addition to learning the jobs of each system and the organs that help carry out these vital functions, the children also learned many new vocabulary words. Help your child to make these words a part of his or her own vocabulary by using them when you talk together about body systems.

artery
capillary
vein
valve
mucus
trachea
bronchioles
air sacs
esophagus

The following pages include activities that you and your child can do together. By participating in your child's education, you will help to bring the learning home.

Family Science Activity
Pulse and Breath Rate Check

To find your pulse, measure the beat at your wrist for 15 seconds and multiply by 4.
To find your breath rate, count how many times you breathe in 15 seconds and multiply by 4.

Study the connection between the circulatory and respiratory systems with this experiment. Use this chart to check a person's pulse and breath rate before and after doing an aerobic activity, such as running or doing jumping jacks for three minutes. One person will have to do the activity and count his or her pulse and breath rate. The other person will have to keep track of the time and write the results.

	Family Member 1	Family Member 2
Pulse Before Activity		
Breath Rate Before Activity		
Pulse Immediately After Activity		
Breath Rate Immediately After Activity		
Pulse Five Minutes After Activity		
Breath Rate Five Minutes After Activity		

How long did it take your pulse to return to normal?
How long did it take your breath rate to return to normal?
Why do you think your pulse and breath rates increased during exercise?

Workbook

Vocabulary Practice

Structures of Living Things

Unscramble the letters to find the vocabulary words.
Then use the circled letters to answer the riddle
below.

VNIE   _ _ _ ⊙(3)

SUMUC   _ _ _ _ ⊙(7)

VVEAL   _ _ _ _ ⊙(11)

AYERRT   _ _ ⊙(4) _ _ ⊙(5)

TEARHAC   ⊙(2) _ _ _ _ _ ⊙(8)

SAACISR   _ _ _ _ _ _ ⊙(1)

HAEGSUSOP   _ _ _ _ _ _ _ _ _

LCPLIRAYA   _ ⊙(10) _ _ _ _ _ _ _

BHLEIROSONC   _ _ ⊙(9) _ _ _ _ _ _ ⊙(6) _

© Pearson Education, Inc.

What instrument helps a doctor check the health
of your respiratory system?

A ⊙⊙⊙⊙⊙⊙⊙⊙⊙⊙⊙
1 2 3 4 5 6 7 8 9 10 11

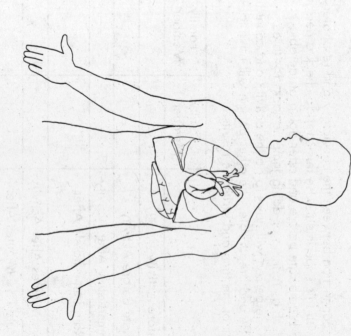

Fun Fact

The average child has about 60,000 miles of
blood vessels!

Look through the chapter to find a definition and a
picture for each vocabulary word. Draw a simple sketch
that illustrates the word and write its definition.

Vocabulary Word	Simple Sketch	Definition of the Word
pollen		
pollination		
photosynthesis		
xylem		
phloem		
tropism		
growth hormone		
embryo		
spore		

Notes for Home: Your child learned the vocabulary words for Chapter 4.
Home Activity: In random order, say the definitions of the vocabulary words, and
have your child give the correct vocabulary words.

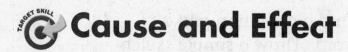
Cause and Effect

Read the science story. Think about causes and effects.

A Dying Maple Tree

Carol decided to observe the changes to a maple tree in her backyard during one summer. She looked at its appearance and its growth and tried to figure out if it was healthy or not. She recorded the number of days the tree was watered by rain and the number of days the tree received sunlight. She figured that since it rained every few days, and the tree produced large, green leaves, the tree must be getting enough water and sun and therefore was healthy.

One night, there was a terrible thunderstorm. Carol looked at the maple tree the next day and saw that many of its leaves and even some of its bark had fallen off. She knew that the bark of a tree helps protect it from disease and bugs. She watched the maple tree very closely in the next few weeks.

Carol noticed that there were lots of bugs crawling on the maple tree. Then she saw that there were many small holes in the trunk of the maple tree. She told her parents. They had a tree specialist inspect the maple tree. The tree specialist told Carol and her parents that the tree was dying.

Apply It!

Fill in the graphic organizer with causes and effects you found in the science story on page 32.

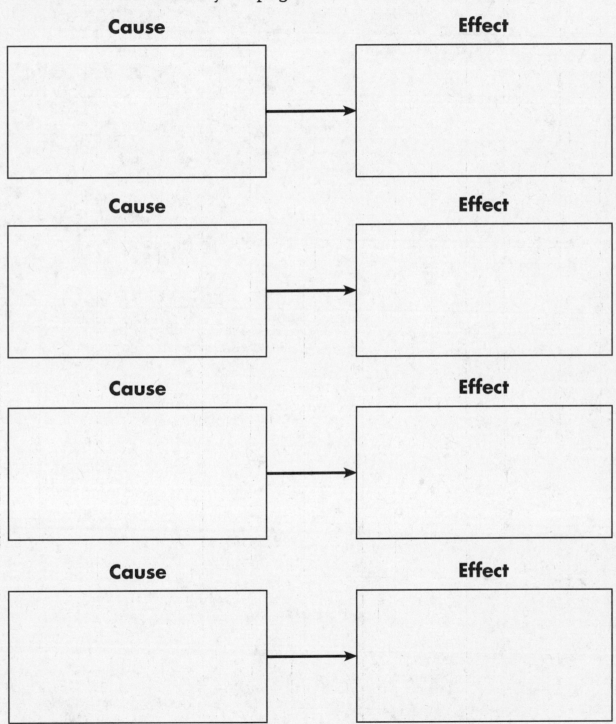

Cause

Effect

Cause

Effect

Cause

Effect

Cause

Effect

Notes for Home: Your child learned to identify causes and effects.
Home Activity: Discuss with your child what might cause a plant to die. Then discuss what the effects on people would be if the plants on Earth began to die.

Notes

Lesson 1: How do leaves help a plant?

Before You Read Lesson 1

Read each statement below. Place a check mark in the circle to indicate whether you agree or disagree with the statement.

		Agree	Disagree
1.	Cells and tissues make up leaves.	○	○
2.	Leaves have an outside epidermis that protects the plant.	○	○
3.	Chloroplasts are in plant and animal cells.	○	○
4.	A plant uses oxygen to make carbon dioxide during photosynthesis.	○	○

After You Read Lesson 1

Reread each statement above. If the lesson supports your choice, place a check mark in the *Correct* circle. Then explain how the text supports your choice. If the lesson does not support your choice, place a check mark in the *Incorrect* circle. Then explain why your choice is wrong.

		Correct	Incorrect
1.	_____	○	○
	_____		
2.	_____	○	○
	_____		
3.	_____	○	○
	_____		
4.	_____	○	○
	_____		

Notes for Home: Your child has completed a pre/post inventory of key concepts in the lesson.
Home Activity: With your child, look for different kinds of leaves. Ask your child to explain the process of photosynthesis that occurs in leaves.

Reviewing Terms: Matching

Match each description with the correct word. Write the letter on the line next to the description.

_____ 1. the outside layer of flat cells in a
            plant leaf

_____ 2. the type of tissue that carries food
            and water through a plant

_____ 3. the process that plants use to make
            sugar for food

_____ 4. material made of thousands of
            sugars for cell walls of plants

a. cellulose

b. vessel tissue

c. epidermis

d. photosynthesis

Reviewing Concepts: Sentence Completion

Complete each sentence with the correct word or phrase.

_____ 5. Leaves are _____ in plants. (tissues, organs)

_____ 6. Plants _____ use cellular respiration. (do, do not)

_____ 7. _____ is the long-term storage product in
                     plants. (Sugar, Starch)

_____ 8. Photosynthesis requires sunlight, water, and
                     _____. (oxygen, carbon dioxide)

Applying Strategies: Cause and Effect

Use complete sentences to answer question 9. (2 points)

9. For a science fair experiment, you decide to test a certain type of
    plant to see how well it can grow when it is kept out of sunlight.
    For two weeks, the plant leaves stay green then they begin to look
    yellow. Use the terms *photosynthesis, sunshine, energy, stored food,* and
    sugar to describe what is happening to the plant.

    _____

    _____

    _____

© Pearson Education, Inc.

Name _____

Lesson 2: How do stems and roots help a plant?

Before You Read Lesson 2

Read each statement below. Place a check mark in the circle to indicate whether you agree or disagree with the statement.

		Agree	Disagree
1.	All plants have xylem and phloem.	○	○
2.	Xylem carries sugar from the leaves to the other parts of the plant.	○	○
3.	Woody stems have more xylem than soft stems.	○	○
4.	Two types of root systems are the taproot and the fibrous.	○	○

After You Read Lesson 2

Reread each statement above. If the lesson supports your choice, place a check mark in the *Correct* circle. Then explain how the text supports your choice. If the lesson does not support your choice, place a check mark in the *Incorrect* circle. Then explain why your choice is wrong.

		Correct	Incorrect
1.	_____	○	○
	_____		
2.	_____	○	○
	_____		
3.	_____	○	○
	_____		
4.	_____	○	○
	_____		

Notes for Home: Your child has completed a pre/post inventory of key concepts in the lesson.
Home Activity: Have your child explain to you the purposes of stems and roots in plants.

Reviewing Terms: Sentence Completion

Complete each sentence with the correct term.

xylem   phloem   stems   roots

_____ 1. Leaves of plants are attached to organs called
                           _____.

_____ 2. Sugar is carried away from leaves in _____
                           tissues.

_____ 3. Plants are anchored and held in place in the
                           ground by _____.

_____ 4. Water and minerals travel through _____ tubes
                           from the roots to the leaves.

Reviewing Concepts: True or False

Write **T** (True) or **F** (False) on the line before each statement.

_____ 5. Xylem and phloem are found only in roots and stems.

_____ 6. Dead phloem makes up bark.

_____ 7. Taproots divide into many smaller and smaller roots and
              grow out in all directions.

_____ 8. Water enters plants through root hairs.

Writing

Write complete sentences to answer question 9. (2 points)

9. Summarize the functions of roots.

   _____

   _____

   _____

   _____

   _____

Lesson 3: How do plants reproduce?

Before You Read Lesson 3

Read each statement below. Place a check mark in the circle to indicate whether you agree or disagree with the statement.

	Agree	Disagree
1. The stamen is the female part of the flower, and the pistil is the male part.	○	○
2. Pollination can occur in a single plant or between two plants.	○	○
3. Food is stored in seeds.	○	○
4. Seeds and spores both have multicellular embryos.	○	○

After You Read Lesson 3

Reread each statement above. If the lesson supports your choice, place a check mark in the *Correct* circle. Then explain how the text supports your choice. If the lesson does not support your choice, place a check mark in the *Incorrect* circle. Then explain why your choice is wrong.

	Correct	Incorrect
1. _____	○	○
_____		
2. _____	○	○
_____		
3. _____	○	○
_____		
4. _____	○	○
_____		

Notes for Home: Your child has completed a pre/post inventory of key concepts in the lesson.
Home Activity: Look at several flowers with your child, outside, at the grocery store, or at a flower shop. Have your child explain to you the parts of the flower.

Name _____

Reviewing Terms: Matching

Match each description with the correct term. Write the letter of the term on the line next to each description.

_____ 1. movement of pollen from the stamen to the pistil of a plant

_____ 2. a new plant protected by a seed coat

_____ 3. a single plant cell that will develop into a new plant

_____ 4. a grainy yellow powder made at the top of each stamen

a. pollen
b. pollination
c. spore
d. embryo

Reviewing Concepts: Sentence Completion

Complete each sentence with the correct word.

_____ 5. The _____ is the female part of a flower. (stamen, pistil)

_____ 6. Sexual reproduction requires the passing of DNA from _____ parent(s) to their offspring. (one, two)

_____ 7. The seeds of plants with one cotyledon are _____. (monocots, dicots)

_____ 8. In asexual reproduction, _____ of the genetic information comes from one parent. (all, some)

Applying Strategies: Find a Percentage

9. A farmer planted 12,000 corn seeds. Ninety-two percent of the seeds developed into plants. How many plants did the farmer grow? (Show your work.) (2 points)

Name _____

Lesson 4: How do plants grow?

Before You Read Lesson 4

Read each statement below. Place a check mark in the circle to indicate whether you agree or disagree with the statement.

		Agree	Disagree
1.	The shape of a plant is determined by its DNA.	○	○
2.	Plants cannot change the direction they grow because it is part of their DNA.	○	○
3.	Growth hormone is made by plants.	○	○
4.	There is only one kind of tropism that plants experience.	○	○

After You Read Lesson 4

Reread each statement above. If the lesson supports your choice, place a check mark in the *Correct* circle. Then explain how the text supports your choice. If the lesson does not support your choice, place a check mark in the *Incorrect* circle. Then explain why your choice is wrong.

		Correct	Incorrect
1.	_____	○	○
	_____		
2.	_____	○	○
	_____		
3.	_____	○	○
	_____		
4.	_____	○	○
	_____		

Notes for Home: Your child has completed a pre/post inventory of key concepts in the lesson.
Home Activity: Help your child research a common plant that grows in each region of the United States. Have your child compare and contrast the plants.

Name _____

Reviewing Terms: Matching

Match each definition or example with the correct term. Write the letter on the line next to the definition or example.

_____ 1. ways that plants change their direction of growth in response to the environment

_____ 2. a chemical that affects plant growth

_____ 3. when roots grow downward as a result of gravity

_____ 4. a plant's growth response to touching an object

a. tropism

b. growth hormone

Reviewing Concepts: Sentence Completion

Complete each sentence with the correct word.

_____ 5. Growth of a vine around a post is an example of _____. (gravitropism, thigmotropism)

_____ 6. Growth hormones can make cells grow _____. (larger, smaller)

_____ 7. Stems tend to grow _____ the direction of gravity. (in, against)

_____ 8. Plant cells can increase in size when _____ take on water. (vacuoles, nuclei)

Writing

Use complete sentences to answer question 9. (2 points)

9. Janet has a plant with red flowers on her bedroom window sill. Every afternoon when she comes home from school, the plant is facing the window. She has to turn the plant around to see the flowers. Explain why this is happening.

_____

_____

_____

© Pearson Education, Inc.

Name _____

Comparing Plant Growth

A fifth-grade class planted two kinds of bean seeds in the same container so that the seeds are in the same soil and get the same amounts of water and sunlight. The students recorded the heights of the bean plants every seven days. Then they put their data in a bar graph.

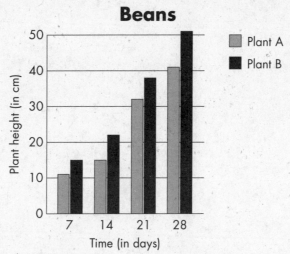

Use the bar graph to answer the questions.

1. After 14 days, how tall was Bean Plant A?
   A. 11 cm   **B.** 15 cm   **C.** 22 cm   **D.** 32 cm

2. Between which days did Bean Plant A grow the fastest?
   A. planting and day 7   **C.** day 14 and day 21
   B. day 7 and day 14   **D.** day 21 and day 28

3. On which day is Bean Plant A about 10 cm shorter than Bean Plant B?
   A. day 7   **B.** day 14   **C.** day 21   **D.** day 28

4. Which is the best estimate of how tall Bean Plant B was on day 19?
   A. 22 cm   **B.** 25 cm   **C.** 36 cm   **D.** 40 cm

5. Which of the following statements is true?
   A. Bean Plant A grew 1 cm each day.
   B. Bean Plant B grew 10 cm every 7 days.
   C. In every 7-day period, the height of Bean Plant B increased by the same amount.
   D. There is no pattern in the growth of either bean plant.

Notes for Home: Your child learned how to read a double bar graph.
Home Activity: With your child, plant two of the same kind of seed but give different amounts of water to each. Record the heights of the plants in a double bar graph.

Notes

Dear Family,

Your child is learning about plants. The class is studying how plants use photosynthesis to make sugar for food. Your child is learning the functions of a plant's leaves, stems, roots, and flowers. The class is also exploring how plants grow and reproduce.

Your child has learned many new vocabulary words that describe plants and their processes. Help your child to make these words a part of his or her own vocabulary by using them when you talk together about body systems.

photosynthesis
xylem
phloem
pollen
pollination
embryo
spore
growth hormone
tropism

The following pages include activities that you and your child can do together. By participating in your child's education, you will help to bring the learning home.

© Pearson Education, Inc.

Family Science Activity
Circulation in Plants

Here's a quick experiment that demonstrates how water and other materials travel throughout a plant.

Materials:

- celery stalk with leafy top (stalks with fresh leaves work best)
- glass of water
- food coloring (red or blue work well)
- knife

Steps:

1. Place three or four drops of food coloring in the glass of water. Then, add the celery stalk.
2. Wait thirty minutes.
3. Notice where the color has entered the celery. This is the celery's xylem. Only the xylem will show the color. You can make the xylem more visible by carefully scraping the stalk with a knife.

Talk About It

Why is the color only in the xylem? Xylem are tubes that carry materials from the roots to the leaves.
What materials are usually carried in the xylem?
Xylem shells are long and shaped like a pipe or straw. Why is this shape useful?

Workbook

Vocabulary Practice

Structures of Living Things

Color in the nine vocabulary words in this puzzle. Then, write the letters that are left over to answer the question.

```
C  P  H  E  L  X
G  H  T  M  P  Y
R  O  R  B  O  L
O  T  O  R  L  E
W  O  P  Y  L  M
T  S  I  O  I  P
H  Y  S  O  N  O
H  N  M  P  A  L
O  T  R  H  T  O
R  H  O  L  I  E
M  E  P  O  O  N
O  S  L  E  N  A
N  I  S  M  T  S
E  S  P  O  R  E
```

Where does photosynthesis happen in a leaf cell?

In the ___ ___ ___ ___ ___ ___ ___ ___ ___ ___ ___ ___.

Answer: chloroplasts

Write the word that completes each sentence. Use letters from the box. Cross off each letter you use. Then rearrange the remaining letters to answer the question.

```
A E E E E F L L L M N N O
O O P R R R S S S S T T V
```

1. Xylem and phloem are found in a plant's ___ ___ ___ ___ ___ ___ ___.

2. A plant's ___ ___ ___ ___ ___ absorb water from the soil and support the plant.

3. Photosynthesis takes place in a plant's ___ ___ ___ ___ ___ ___.

4. ___ ___ ___ ___ ___ ___ is a grainy yellow powder found at the top of flower stamens.

5. A plant ___ ___ ___ ___ is a single plant cell that can develop into a new plant.

What is one kind of plant that can reproduce without seeds? ___ ___ ___ ___.

Fun Fact

Bamboo is a plant. Some kinds of bamboo can grow three feet in one day!

Answers: stem, roots, leaves, pollen, spore, fern.

Workbook

Name _____

Work with a partner to write a definition for each vocabulary word. After you read Chapter 5, look through the chapter to find an example from any biome for each word.

Vocabulary Word	Definition	Example from any biome
ecosystem		
population		
community		
niche		
habitat		
cycle		
energy pyramid		

Notes for Home: Your child learned the vocabulary terms for Chapter 5.
Home Activity: Have your child use the vocabulary words to explain the relationships among communities, populations, and ecosystems.

Predict

Read the science article.

A Balanced Ecosystem

All ecosystems depend on a balance of producers, consumers, and decomposers. A producer is an organism that makes its own food. Grass is a producer. A consumer is an organism that must eat a producer because it cannot make its own food. An example of a consumer is a cow. A decomposer is an organism that eats dead organisms. Worms are decomposers. In some ecosystems, the numbers of producers, consumers, and decomposers can become unbalanced.

Apply It!

Use the graphic organizer on the next page to help you make a prediction. In the right box, write your prediction that answers the question in the left box.

Question

If an unbalanced ecosystem has more consumers than producers, what effects might this have on the decomposers in the ecosystem?

Prediction

© Pearson Education, Inc.

Notes for Home: Your child learned how to make predictions based on scientific information.
Home Activity: With your child predict what might happen if there were no longer any trees. Ask your child what types of plants and animals would be affected.

Notes

Lesson 1: What is an ecosystem?

Before You Read Lesson 1

Read each statement below. Place a check mark in the circle to indicate whether you agree or disagree with the statement.

	Agree	Disagree
1. An ecosystem includes only the living organisms in a given area.	○	○
2. Several different populations can be found in one ecosystem.	○	○
3. A rainforest is an example of a biome.	○	○
4. A niche is where an organism lives in an ecosystem.	○	○

After You Read Lesson 1

Reread each statement above. If the lesson supports your choice, place a check mark in the *Correct* circle. Then explain how the text supports your choice. If the lesson does not support your choice, place a check mark in the *Incorrect* circle. Then explain why your choice is wrong.

	Correct	Incorrect
1. _____ _____	○	○
2. _____ _____	○	○
3. _____ _____	○	○
4. _____ _____	○	○

Notes for Home: Your child has completed a pre/post inventory of key concepts in the lesson.
Home Activity: Have your child compare and contrast the animals and plants that live in two different ecosystems. Help your child make a Venn diagram.

Name _____

Reviewing Terms: Matching

Match each description with the correct term. Write the letter of the term on the line next to the description.

_____ 1. the group of all the populations in an area

_____ 2. the role that an organism has in an ecosystem

_____ 3. the place in which an organism lives

_____ 4. a group of organisms of one species that live in an area at the same time

_____ 5. all the living and nonliving things in an area

a. population
b. habitat
c. ecosystem
d. niche
e. community

Reviewing Concepts: True or False

Write **T** (True) or **F** (False) on the line before each statement.

_____ 5. The air, water, temperature, soil, and sunlight in an ecosystem have no effect on organisms that live in the area.

_____ 6. Ecosystems are everywhere that living things are found.

_____ 7. All the biomes make up the biosphere.

_____ 8. A single biome may be made up of areas around the world that have the same climate and organisms.

Applying Strategies: Predict

Use complete sentences to answer question 9. (2 points)

9. Predict how the niche of trees in a temperate rainforest and the niche of squirrels in the same rainforest interact.

_____

_____

_____

Workbook

Name _____

Lesson 2: What are land biomes?

Before You Read Lesson 2

Read each statement below. Place a check mark in the circle to indicate whether you agree or disagree with the statement.

	Agree	Disagree
1. Tropical rainforests have the largest number of species.	○	○
2. Some animals and plants that can adapt to cold winters live in deciduous forests.	○	○
3. A species's population will never decrease if its habitat changes.	○	○
4. The temperature in desert biomes is always extremely hot.	○	○

After You Read Lesson 2

Reread each statement above. If the lesson supports your choice, place a check mark in the *Correct* circle. Then explain how the text supports your choice. If the lesson does not support your choice, place a check mark in the *Incorrect* circle. Then explain why your choice is wrong.

	Correct	Incorrect
1. _____	○	○
2. _____	○	○
3. _____	○	○
4. _____	○	○

Notes for Home: Your child has completed a pre/post inventory of key concepts in the lesson.
Home Activity: Ask your child to explain how animals adapt to their environments. Have your child tell how he or she has adapted to changes at school or home.

Reviewing Main Ideas: Sentence Completion

Complete each sentence with the correct word or phrase.

_____ 1. Tropical rainforests have _____ species than all other biomes. (more, fewer)

_____ 2. In a _____ trees lose their leaves. (tropical rainforest, deciduous forest)

_____ 3. Grasslands receive little rain and have many types of _____. (trees, grasses)

_____ 4. Most trees in the taiga have needles _____. (throughout the year, only in summer)

_____ 5. A desert is an area that receives _____ 25 centimeters of rain or snow each year. (more than, less than)

_____ 6. A limiting factor in the tundra is _____. (yearly flooding, frozen soil)

Reviewing Concepts: True or False

Write T (True) or F (False) on the line before each statement.

_____ 7. A large root system near the surface is a special structure of some desert plants.

_____ 8. A decrease in rainfall in a tropical rainforest might be a limiting factor for animals and plants living there.

Applying Strategies: Cause and Effect

Use complete sentences to answer question 9. (2 points)

9. Many species of birds leave deciduous forests in the fall. Identify two limiting factors that might cause these animals to go other places.

_____

_____

_____

Name _____

Lesson 3: What are water ecosystems?

Before You Read Lesson 3

Read each statement below. Place a check mark in the circle to indicate whether you agree or disagree with the statement.

	Agree	Disagree
1. The types of plants and animals that live in rivers do not also live in oceans.	○	○
2. Swamps and salt marshes are types of river biomes.	○	○
3 Coral reefs exist in warm, shallow water.	○	○
4. Many plants grow on the floor of deep sea biomes.	○	○

After You Read Lesson 3

Reread each statement above. If the lesson supports your choice, place a check mark in the *Correct* circle. Then explain how the text supports your choice. If the lesson does not support your choice, place a check mark in the *Incorrect* circle. Then explain why your choice is wrong.

	Correct	Incorrect
1. _____ _____	○	○
2. _____ _____	○	○
3. _____ _____	○	○
4. _____ _____	○	○

Notes for Home: Your child has completed a pre/post inventory of key concepts in the lesson.
Home Activity: Help your child create a song about the differences among the water biomes. Use a familiar tune, and ask your child to write the lyrics.

Reviewing Terms: Matching

Match each description with the correct term. Write the letter of the term on the line next to the definition.

_____ 1. a body of water that might flow slow or fast

_____ 2. an area that is partly covered by water or flooded part of each year

_____ 3. a deep body of water with organisms adapted to cold, darkness, and very high water pressure

_____ 4. warm, shallow waters with many organisms

a. coral reef

b. wetland

c. river

d. deep sea

Reviewing Concepts: Sentence Completion

Complete each sentence with the correct word.

_____ 5. Plants cannot grow in the _____ because sunlight cannot reach the cold depths. (coral reef, deep sea)

_____ 6. Usually, plants and animals that live in _____ do not also live in oceans. (rivers, coral reefs)

_____ 7. Coral reefs _____ in water that does not have many nutrients or high levels of oxygen. (grow well, grow poorly)

_____ 8. The plants, soils, and microorganisms of wetlands often _____ the water that flows through them. (clean, pollute)

Writing

Use complete sentences to answer question 9. (2 points)

9. What are salt marshes? How do they differ from swamps?

_____

_____

_____

Name _____

Lesson 4: How do organisms interact?

Before You Read Lesson 4

Read each statement below. Place a check mark in the circle to indicate whether you agree or disagree with the statement.

		Agree	Disagree
1.	Animals in an ecosystem may compete for food or water.	○	○
2.	Plants may compete with each other for sunlight.	○	○
3	In all symbiotic relationships, both species harm each other.	○	○
4.	Parasites are organisms that benefit their hosts.	○	○

After You Read Lesson 4

Reread each statement above. If the lesson supports your choice, place a check mark in the *Correct* circle. Then explain how the text supports your choice. If the lesson does not support your choice, place a check mark in the *Incorrect* circle. Then explain why your choice is wrong.

	Correct	Incorrect
1. _____ _____	○	○
2. _____ _____	○	○
3. _____ _____	○	○
4. _____ _____	○	○

Notes for Home: Your child has completed a pre/post inventory of key concepts in the lesson.
Home Activity: Have your child explain to you why some animals compete with each other. Ask your child to think of ways humans compete with one another.

© Pearson Education, Inc.

Reviewing Terms: Matching

Match each description or example with the correct term. Write the term on the line next to the description.

parasite   competition   host   symbiosis

_____ 1. a long-term relationship between different species

_____ 2. an organism that may or may not be harmed in a relationship

_____ 3. an organism that feeds off another organism and causes it harm

_____ 4. two sheep hitting their horns together

Reviewing Concepts: True or False

Write **T** (True) or **F** (False) on the line before each statement.

_____ 5. Animals compete for resources, but plants do not compete.

_____ 6. In a lichen, only one organism benefits

_____ 7. Microorganisms taking oxygen from an animal's blood are a helpful form of symbiosis.

_____ 8. Kudzu is harmful because it prevents the plants that it covers from getting sunlight.

Applying Strategies: Calculating

9. By 1980, kudzu had covered about 2,833,000 hectares of land. It was covering about 130,000 hectares per year. At that rate, how many total hectares did kudzu cover by the end of the next five years? (2 points)

Name _____

Lesson 5: How does energy move in ecosystems?

Before You Read Lesson 5

Read each statement below. Place a check mark in the circle to indicate whether you agree or disagree with the statement.

		Agree	Disagree
1.	Examples of producers include carnivores and herbivores.	○	○
2.	Omnivores eat plants and animals.	○	○
3	Consumers have the greatest amount of energy in an ecosystem.	○	○
4.	The organisms at the top of the energy pyramid have the least amount of energy.	○	○

After You Read Lesson 5

Reread each statement above. If the lesson supports your choice, place a check mark in the *Correct* circle. Then explain how the text supports your choice. If the lesson does not support your choice, place a check mark in the *Incorrect* circle. Then explain why your choice is wrong.

		Correct	Incorrect
1.	_____	○	○
	_____		
2.	_____	○	○
	_____		
3.	_____	○	○
	_____		
4.	_____	○	○
	_____		

Notes for Home: Your child has completed a pre/post inventory of key concepts in the lesson.
Home Activity: Have your child draw an energy pyramid. Ask your child to explain the levels of the pyramid.

Name _____

Reviewing Terms: Matching

Match each description with the correct term. Write the letter of the term on the line next to the description.

_____ 1. organisms that make their own food

_____ 2. organisms that usually eat other organisms to get energy

_____ 3. organisms that eat waste or dead organisms

_____ 4. a diagram that shows the amounts of energy that flow through each level of a food chain

_____ 5. what most energy from food turns into

a. consumers

b. decomposers

c. energy pyramid

d. body heat

e. producers

Reviewing Concepts: Sentence Completion

Complete each sentence with the correct word or phrase.

_____ 6. All _____ are consumers. (plants, animals)

_____ 7. Energy can flow through an ecosystem from a producer to a(n) _____. (producer, herbivore)

_____ 8. Energy _____ disappear. (does, does not)

Applying Strategies: Sequence

9. Draw a food chain that shows the relationships among the following animals: grass, hawk, mouse, and snake. Label each as a producer or a consumer. (2 points)

© Pearson Education, Inc.

Name _____

Lesson 6: What cycles occur in ecosystems?

Before You Read Lesson 6

Read each statement below. Place a check mark in the circle to indicate whether you agree or disagree with the statement.

	Agree	Disagree
1. Banana slugs and slime molds are both decomposers.	○	○
2. Most plants and animals get nitrogen from the air.	○	○
3 Decomposers are not part of the nitrogen cycle.	○	○
4. Carbon dioxide is a product of respiration and combustion.	○	○

After You Read Lesson 6

Reread each statement above. If the lesson supports your choice, place a check mark in the *Correct* circle. Then explain how the text supports your choice. If the lesson does not support your choice, place a check mark in the *Incorrect* circle. Then explain why your choice is wrong.

	Correct	Incorrect
1. _____ _____	○	○
2. _____ _____	○	○
3. _____ _____	○	○
4. _____ _____	○	○

Notes for Home: Your child has completed a pre/post inventory of key concepts in the lesson.
Home Activity: With your child, investigate the recycling program in your town or state. Ask your child how this program is similar to the scientific cycles covered in the lesson.

Reviewing Main Ideas: Sentence Completion

Complete each sentence with the correct word or phrase.

_____ 1. The role of _____ is to recycle wastes and dead material. (consumers, decomposers)

_____ 2. There is a constant _____ of minerals and some nutrients moving from living things to the soil and back into living things. (cycle, niche)

_____ 3. Most organisms _____ use nitrogen gas from the air. (can, cannot)

_____ 4. Some sources of nitrogen compounds are _____ and fertilizer. (carbon dioxide, lightning)

_____ 5. The most abundant gas in the atmosphere is _____. (oxygen, nitrogen)

_____ 6. Oxygen can enter the atmosphere during _____. (cellular respiration, photosynthesis)

_____ 7. One result of combustion is _____. (oxygen, carbon dioxide)

_____ 8. The results of respiration are carbon dioxide and _____. (water, oxygen)

Writing

Use complete sentences to answer question 9. (2 points)

9. Why are decomposers important to other living things?

_____

_____

_____

_____

_____

_____

Name _____

The Logistic Model of Growth

The graph below is called the Logistic Growth Model. It shows the rate at which a cold virus spreads within a class of 25 students. First, only one student is infected, and so the cold virus has a large number of potential victims. At this point, the cold is spreading very quickly. As more and more students get sick, the number of potential new victims decreases and so does the rate of infection until every student has the cold.

Logistic Growth Model

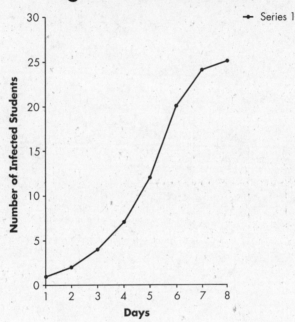

Use the graph to answer the following questions.

1. About how many students had the cold on day 1? _____

2. About how many students had the cold on day 6? _____

3. About how many new students caught the cold from day 4 to day 6? _____

4. By which day was the entire class sick? _____

Notes for Home: Your child learned about scientific models.
Home Activity: Using an almanac, help your child plot a graph about the U.S. population between 1930 and 2000. Ask your child if the graph looks similar to the logistic growth model.

Notes

Dear Family,

Your child is learning about interactions in ecosystems, which include all the living and nonliving things in an area. The class is studying varieties of land biomes, from tropical rain forests to deserts, as well as water ecosystems from wetlands to coral reefs. Your child is studying the relationships within ecosystems, such as competition between animals for limited resources. The class is also looking at the cycles in ecosystems, including the movement of energy in food webs and the nitrogen cycle.

Your child has learned many new vocabulary words that describe ecosystems. Help your child to make these words a part of his or her own vocabulary by using them when you talk together about environments near and far.

ecosystem
population
community
niche
habitat
energy pyramid
cycle

The following pages include activities that you and your child can do together. By participating in your child's education, you will help to bring the learning home.

Family Science Activity
Ecosystem Card Deck

Materials:

- index cards
- markers, crayons
- magazines

Steps

Choose one of these land biomes and create a deck of cards showing organisms that live there:

tropical rain forest   deciduous rain forest   grassland
taiga   desert   tundra

① Work with a family team to brainstorm a list of organisms that live in this biome. Remember to include plants, insects, and decomposers, like bacteria and worms. Write the name of one organism on each index card.

② Write facts about each animal, including information about its diet and habitat. Classify animals as herbivores, carnivores, or omnivores. Use reference books or Internet sources for more information.

③ Add illustrations, or photographs from magazines to illustrate each organism.

Invent your own games such as using the cards to play charades. You can also post the cards on a bulletin board and use arrows to create a food web for the biome you explored.

Interactions in Ecosystems

Write the vocabulary word that completes each sentence. Then use the numbered letters to find the puzzle answer.

1. Every organism has its own __ __ __ __ __ , or
role in an ecosystem.   13   2

2. You can look at an energy __ __ __ __ __ __
to see the amounts of energy that flow through   6
each level of a food chain.

3. A __ __ __ __ __ __ __ __ is a
group of organisms of one species that live in an   8
area at the same time.

4. The place where an organisms lives is its
__ __ __ __ __ __ __ .

5. A __ __ __ __ __ __ __ __ __ is all of the
       7   5
populations in an area.

6. There is a constant __ __ __ __ __ of minerals
                        11   9
moving from living things to the soil and back
into living things.

7. An __ __ __ __ __ __ __ __ __ includes all
       15   3   10   12
of the living and nonliving things in an area.

There's no light in a deep-sea ecosystem, but
some animals can make their own! What is the
production of light by living animals called?

__ __ __ __ __ __ __ __ __ __ __ __ __ __ __
1   2   3   4   5   6   7   8   9 10 11 12 13 14 15

Fun Fact

The driest desert biome is the Atacama Desert in
South America. Some parts of this desert haven't
had rain in 400 years! The wettest place on
Earth is Meghalaya in India. It rains an average
of 1,270 cm there each year. Once it rained
2,290 cm in a single season!

Answers: 1. niche; 2. pyramid; 3. population; 4. habitat; 5. community; 6. cycle; 7. ecosystem

Answer: bioluminescence

In the first box, write what you think the vocabulary word means. After you finish reading the chapter, write two examples for each vocabulary word in the second and third boxes.

(inherit)

Meaning

Example

Example

(mutation)

Meaning

Example

Example

(pesticide)

Meaning

Example

Example

(structural adaptation)

Meaning

Example

Example

(behavioral adaptation)

Meaning

Example

Example

(extinct)

Meaning

Example

Example

Notes for Home: Your child learned the vocabulary terms for Chapter 6.
Home Activity: Have your child use the vocabulary words to explain the difference between a structural adaptation and a behavioral adaptation.

Cause and Effect

Read the newspaper article.

European Starlings

European starlings were introduced to the ecosystems of North America in 1890. Since then, their numbers have grown from about 100 birds to approximately 200,000,000. Scientists believe there are several reasons why the European starling population has grown so quickly.

First, European starlings can easily live with humans. They build their nests in city locations. Second, European starlings have a special bill that makes it easy for them to find food in thick grass. Other species of birds must compete for resources with European starlings. Some birds lose their homes as a result.

Apply It!

Fill in the graphic organizer. List causes and effects from the article on page 54.

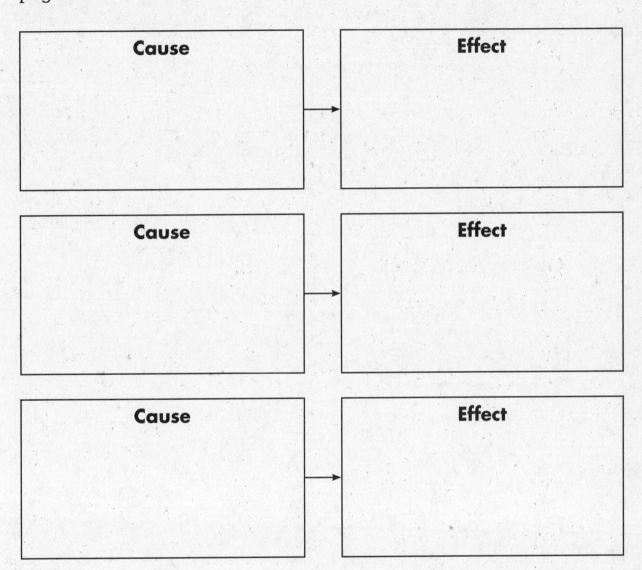

| **Cause** | | **Effect** |
| | → | |

| **Cause** | | **Effect** |
| | → | |

| **Cause** | | **Effect** |
| | → | |

Notes for Home: Your child learned about causes and effects.
Home Activity: Have your child name the cause and effect of certain household events. For example, what is the cause and effect if garbage is not removed from the household?

Notes

Lesson 1: How do ecosystems change?

Before You Read Lesson 1

Read each statement below. Place a check mark in the circle to indicate whether you agree or disagree with the statement.

		Agree	Disagree
---	---	:-::	:-:
1.	Ecosystems can be changed by humans as well as forces of nature.	○	○
2.	When people introduce new animals or plants into an ecosystem, it changes.	○	○
3.	The garbage in landfills decays quickly.	○	○
4.	Acid rain is caused by water pollution.	○	○

After You Read Lesson 1

Reread each statement above. If the lesson supports your choice, place a check mark in the *Correct* circle. Then explain how the text supports your choice. If the lesson does not support your choice, place a check mark in the *Incorrect* circle. Then explain why your choice is wrong.

		Correct	Incorrect
1.	_____	○	○
	_____		
2.	_____	○	○
	_____		
3.	_____	○	○
	_____		
4.	_____	○	○
	_____		

Notes for Home: Your child has completed a pre/post inventory of key concepts in the lesson.
Home Activity: Help your child think of ways to reduce the garbage your family throws away every day. Together make a list of helpful hints you can use.

Name _____

Lesson 1 Review

Use with pages 167–169.

Reviewing Concepts: Sentence Completion

Complete each sentence with the correct term.

acid rain   harmful   helpful   landfills

_____ 1. Earthworms are _____ to soil when they dig holes and bring oxygen to plant roots.

_____ 2. Soils and lakes affected by _____ can change ecosystems.

_____ 3. Swarms of feeding locusts can be _____ to farm fields.

_____ 4. Liners in _____ seal off garbage to keep harmful chemicals from leaking into the ground.

Reviewing Concepts: True or False

Write **T** (True) or **F** (False) on the line before each statement.

_____ 5. Organisms, wind, or water can change ecosystems.

_____ 6. Every change that occurs in an ecosystem is harmful.

_____ 7. People change ecosystems when they clear forests.

_____ 8. Organisms without predators harm an ecosystem.

Writing

Use complete sentences to answer question 9. (2 points)

9. What are two ways new species of organisms can be introduced to an ecosystem? Give an example of a species that has been introduced to the United States and tell what its effect has been.

_____

_____

_____

_____

_____

© Pearson Education, Inc.

56A Lesson Review

Workbook

Lesson 2: How do species change?

Before You Read Lesson 2

Read each statement below. Place a check mark in the circle to indicate whether you agree or disagree with the statement.

	Agree	Disagree
1. Every animal inherits the same mix of genes from its parents.	○	○
2. The environment does not affect a species's appearance.	○	○
3. A hummingbird's long beak is a structural adaptation.	○	○
4. Adaptations to an environment can help a species live longer.	○	○

After You Read Lesson 2

Reread each statement above. If the lesson supports your choice, place a check mark in the *Correct* circle. Then explain how the text supports your choice. If the lesson does not support your choice, place a check mark in the *Incorrect* circle. Then explain why your choice was wrong.

	Correct	Incorrect
1. _____	○	○
_____		
2. _____	○	○
_____		
3. _____	○	○
_____		
4. _____	○	○
_____		

Notes for Home: Your child has completed a pre/post inventory of key concepts in the lesson.
Home Activity: Ask your child to think of ways that people adapt to their environments as they grow older. Together make a list.

Reviewing Terms: Sentence Completion

Complete each sentence with the correct term.

_____ 1. Plants and animals _____ half of the genes from each parent in the process of heredity. (mutate, inherit)

_____ 2. A _____ is a body part that helps an organism survive in its ecosystem. (mutation, structural adaptation)

_____ 3. A changed gene is called a(n) _____. (mutation, adaptation)

_____ 4. Inherited behaviors that help animals survive are called _____. (structural adaptations, behavioral adaptations)

Reviewing Concepts: True or False

Write **T** (True) or **F** (False) on the line before each statement.

_____ 5. Almost everything about how an organism grows is determined by its genes.

_____ 6. Some traits are the result of the environment.

_____ 7. Organisms with adaptations to compete for limited resources may survive and pass their genes to their offspring.

_____ 8. Natural selection happens when an adaptation has been inherited by just a few members of a population.

Applying Strategies: Compare and Contrast

Use complete sentences to answer question 9. (2 points)

9. How are instincts and learned behaviors alike and different?

_____

_____

_____

© Pearson Education, Inc.

Lesson 3: How do changes cause more changes?

Before You Read Lesson 3

Read each statement below. Place a check mark in the circle to indicate whether you agree or disagree with the statement.

		Agree	Disagree
1.	Organisms can adapt to harmful changes in their ecosystem.	○	○
2.	Once organisms lose their habitats, they can never find new homes.	○	○
3.	An extinct species has limited numbers of its kind.	○	○
4.	Poisons in ecosystems can travel through the food chain.	○	○

After You Read Lesson 3

Reread each statement above. If the lesson supports your choice, place a check mark in the *Correct* circle. Then explain how the text supports your choice. If the lesson does not support your choice, place a check mark in the *Incorrect* circle. Then explain why your choice was wrong.

		Correct	Incorrect
1.	_____	○	○
	_____		
2.	_____	○	○
	_____		
3.	_____	○	○
	_____		
4.	_____	○	○
	_____		

Notes for Home: Your child has completed a pre/post inventory of key concepts in the lesson.
Home Activity: Have your child draw a diagram to show the idea of natural selection. Choose a species in your area that has survived a change in its environment.

Reviewing Terms: Matching

Match each definition or example with the correct term. Write the letter on the line next to the definition or example.

_____ 1. poisons that kill insects

_____ 2. a species that has no members of its kind alive

_____ 3. sources of evidence about past extinctions

    a. extinct

    b. fossils

    c. pesticides

Reviewing Main Ideas: Sentence Completion

Complete each sentence with the correct word or phrase.

_____ 4. Some populations of mosquitoes have developed _____ to changes in their ecosystem. (pesticides, adaptations)

_____ 5. Medicines used to kill disease-causing bacteria are called _____. (antibiotics, pesticides)

_____ 6. When bacteria develop adaptations, diseases become _____ to treat. (harder, easier)

_____ 7. Scientists use _____ to learn about past extinctions. (fossils, living dodos)

_____ 8. Bald eagles began to die out when _____ washed into lakes and streams. (DDT, DNA)

Applying Strategies: Calculating

9. The dodo became extinct around the year 1680. How many years have passed since the dodo became extinct? Show your work. (2 points)

Endangered Animal Species

As of December 2001, the U.S. Fish and Wildlife Service listed 988 endangered species. Of these, 599 are plant species. The other 389 are animal species, and they are grouped into five categories.

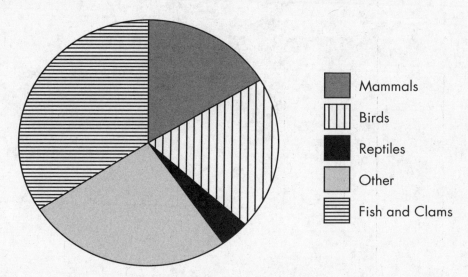

Mammals
Birds
Reptiles
Other
Fish and Clams

Use the circle graph to answer these questions.

1. Added together, mammals, birds, fish, and clams represent about what percent of all listed endangered animal species?
    A. 25%   C. 70%
    B. 50%   D. 95%

2. The category *Other* includes amphibians, arachnids, insects, snails, and crustaceans. What percentage of endangered animal species do these animals total?
    A. 25%   C. 75%
    B. 50%   D. 100%

3. Which category contains the largest number of endangered animal species?
    A. Mammals   C. Birds
    B. Fish and Clams   D. Reptiles

Notes for Home: Your child has learned how to interpret a circle graph.
Home Activity: Help your child make a circle graph that shows the time he or she spends on various activities during a typical day. Remember that the percents should add up to 100%.

Notes

Dear Family,

Your child is learning about the reasons ecosystems change. The class explored how the activities of animals and humans created significant changes in their surroundings. The class looked at how species change as genes are passed from parent to child, and some mutations lead to helpful adaptations. These changes can lead to changes in populations, such as the development of bacteria that resist antibiotics. Species can also become extinct, or die out completely.

Your child has learned the following vocabulary words to talk about changing ecosystems. Help your child to make these words a part of his or her own vocabulary by using them when you talk together about body systems.

inherit
mutation
pesticide
structural adaptation
behavioral adaptation
extinct

The following pages include activities that you and your child can do together. By participating in your child's education, you will help to bring the learning home.

Family Science Activity
Chain of Changes

Try this game whenever you and your child have some free time, such as walking to school or driving to a ballgame. Here is an example of the start for a Chain of Changes:

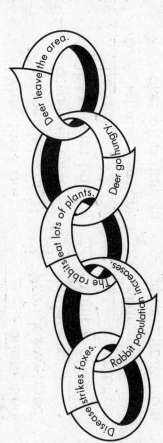

1. One player begins by naming an ecosystem. For example, you might select a local pond or lake, a desert, a rain forest, a swamp, or a grassland.
2. Both players should share ideas about what the ecosystem is like, including the kinds of plants and animals that live there.
3. The next player describes one change in the ecosystem. The other player then describes another change that happens as a result. After several turns, look back at the many ways the ecosystem has changed.
4. At home, you and your child can create a paper chain illustrating the changes. Write one change on a strip of paper and tape it into a ring. Write the resulting change on the next paper link.

Discuss how one small change can lead to large changes in an ecosystem.

Changes in Ecosystems

Find the vocabulary word that completes each sentence. Write the words to complete the puzzle.

Answers: 1. behavioral; 2. structural; 3. inherit; 4. mutation; 5. extinct; 6. adapt

Across

4. A _____ is any change that happens in an organism's genes.
5. When there are no members of a species alive, the species has become _____.
6. A helpful mutation makes an organism _____ to better fit in their parents.

Down

1. The way penguins huddle together to stay warm is an example of a _____ adaptation.
2. A duck's webbed feet are an example of a _____ adaptation.
3. Children _____ genetic traits from their parents.
   an ecosystem.

Fun Fact

The cormorant is a bird that has developed a behavioral adaptation to make sure the kids get out of the house. When the mother thinks the young birds are ready to leave home, she completely destroys the nest!

Workbook

Read each definition below and then use the vocabulary
word in a sentence.

1. Scientists measure how much salt is in water. This is called salinity.
    Use the word *salinity* in a sentence.

    _____

    _____

2. An aquifer is the rock and soil layer in which groundwater is able
    to flow through.
    Use the word *aquifer* in a sentence.

    _____

    _____

3. Reservoirs are lakes that have formed behind dams.
    Use the word *reservoir* in a sentence.

    _____

    _____

4. Sleet is raindrops that are frozen.
    Use the word *sleet* in a sentence.

    _____

    _____

The following vocabulary words all have to do with the water cycle.
Use your textbook to review their definitions. Then draw a line from
the vocabulary word to its correct definition.

Precipitation   water changes from its liquid form into water
                       vapor

Evaporation   ice becomes water vapor without melting first

Condensation   rain, snow, hail, and sleet that fall from clouds

Sublimation   water vapor changes into liquid

Notes for Home: Your child learned the vocabulary terms for Chapter 7.
Home Activity: Use the vocabulary terms to create a crossword puzzle. Have your
child write the definitions for each term to use as clues for the puzzle.

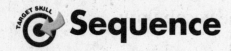
Sequence

Students in a fifth grade science class conducted an experiment to observe what happens to a glass when it is placed upside down on the grass in the sunshine.

Lab Report

Procedure	Observations
Place a clean glass upside down on grass in the Sun.	The water from the soil is evaporating.
Allow the glass to sit on the grass for several minutes.	Water drops are forming on the inside of the glass.

Interpret Results

The water in the soil was evaporating into the air. Since the glass was placed on the grass, the water vapor became trapped inside it. The students were able to see water droplets on the glass in the form of condensation.

Apply It!

Use the graphic organizer below to rewrite the information from the experiment on page 64. Place the information in the correct sequence.

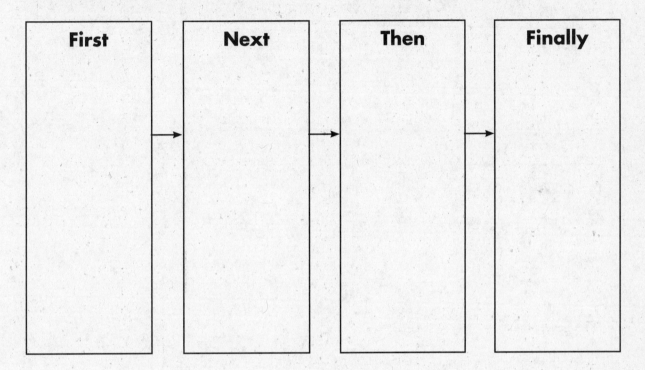

First	Next	Then	Finally

Notes for Home: Your child learned how to put scientific information into sequential order.
Home Activity: Have your child use sequence words (such as *first, next,* and *last*) to explain why water forms on the outside of a cold drink.

Notes

Name _____

Lesson 1: How can the oceans be described?

Before You Read Lesson 1

Read each statement below. Place a check mark in the circle to indicate whether you agree or disagree with the statement.

	Agree	Disagree
1. Oceans cover about 75 percent of the entire Earth.	O	O
2. The salinity of all the world's oceans is exactly the same.	O	O
3. Rivers deliver salt to the oceans.	O	O
4. As you travel north, the temperature of the ocean always gets colder.	O	O

After You Read Lesson 1

Reread each statement above. If the lesson supports your choice, place a check mark in the *Correct* circle. Then explain how the text supports your choice. If the lesson does not support your choice, place a check mark in the *Incorrect* circle. Then explain why your choice is wrong.

	Correct	Incorrect
1. _____	O	O
2. _____	O	O
3. _____	O	O
4. _____	O	O

Notes for Home: Your child has completed a pre/post inventory of key concepts in the lesson.
Home Activity: With your child, find out more about the world's saltiest bodies of water, like the Great Salt Lake and the Dead Sea.

© Pearson Education, Inc.

Name _____

Reviewing Terms: Matching

Match each term with the correct description. Write the letter of the description on the line next to the term.

_____ 1. hydrosphere   **a.** a measure of how salty water is

_____ 2. sodium chloride   **b.** all the waters of Earth

_____ 3. salinity   **c.** common table salt

Reviewing Concepts: True or False

Write **T** (True) or **F** (False) on the line before each statement.

_____ 4. Ocean water makes up only a small part of the hydrosphere.

_____ 5. The Atlantic Ocean is the deepest ocean on Earth.

_____ 6. Places where rivers pour fresh water into the ocean have low salinity.

_____ 7. The Gulf Stream is a current that carries warm water northward.

_____ 8. Ocean water is made drinkable by adding salt.

Applying Concepts: Calculate

9. As of July 2004, the population of the United States was 293,027,571. If more than half of these people live within 80 kilometers of an ocean, about how many people live within that distance? Show your work. (2 points)

© Pearson Education, Inc.

_____

ɔn 4: How do clouds form?

Be̶ You Read Lesson 4

Rea̶ h statement below. Place a check mark in the circle to indicate
wheth̶ ɔu agree or disagree with the statement.

	Agree	Disagree
1. W̶ droplets and ice crystals make up	○	○
2. W̶s clouds are seen higher than cumulus clouds.	○	○
3 ɪs a type of cloud at ground level.	○	○
ᵢ is the same as hail.	○	○
4. V̶		

ou Read Lesson 4

ᵉach statement above. If the lesson supports your choice, place
Aft̶ mark in the *Correct* circle. Then explain how the text supports
Rerᵉ oice. If the lesson does not support your choice, place a check
a chᵤ the *Incorrect* circle. Then explain why your choice is wrong.
you̶
mo̶

	Correct	Incorrect
_____	○	○
_____		
2. _____	○	○
_____		
3. _____	○	○
_____		
4. _____	○	○
_____		

Notes for Home: Your child has completed a pre/post inventory of key concepts in the lesson.
Home Activity: Take a walk with your child outside. Have your child identify several different types of clouds.

Reviewing Terms: Matching

Match each definition with the correct term. Write the letter on the line next to the definition.

_____ 1. frozen raindrops

_____ 2. rain that freezes as soon as it hits a cold object

_____ 3. water vapor that changes into tiny water droplets or ice crystals

a. cloud

b. sleet

c. freezing rain

Reviewing Concepts: Sentence Completion

Complete each sentence with the correct word or phrase.

_____ 4. Cloud formation depends on temperature and _____. (rainfall, air pressure)

_____ 5. _____ clouds form above 6,000 meters. (Cirrus, Stratus)

_____ 6. A cloud that forms at ground level is called _____. (fog, lenticular)

_____ 7. Clouds that grow vertically with rising air inside are _____ clouds. (altocumulus, thunderhead)

_____ 8. The temperature of the air high above the ground is often _____ 0°C. (above, below)

Applying Strategies: Sequence

Use complete sentences to answer question 9. (2 points)

9. Sequence the steps in the formation of hail.

_____

_____

_____

_____

_____

Estimating Area

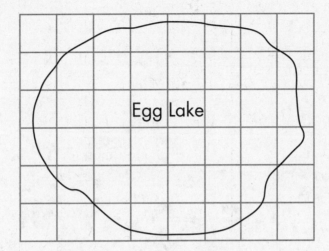

An outline of Egg Lake seen in a grid system allows you to estimate its area. Each square in the grid system represents an area of one square kilometer. Use the following steps to estimate the surface area of Egg Lake.

1. Look at the diagram of the lake.

2. Count the number of squares that are completely enclosed within the lake. How many of these squares are there?

   _____

3. Count the number of squares in the rectangle. How many squares are in this rectangle?

   _____

4. Find the average of the number of squares in steps 2 and 3. Now, what is the estimated area of the lake?

   _____

Notes for Home: Your child has learned how to estimate the area of an irregular figure.
Home Activity: Trace the outline of an oval serving dish onto a grid system and use the steps above to estimate its area. Use a grid system whose squares are all one centimeter in length.

Notes

Dear Family,

Your child is learning about water on Earth. In the science chapter Water on Earth, we studied where fresh water is found and how it gets to our homes, schools, and businesses. We also learned about the water cycle, the repeated movement of water through the environment in different forms, such as water vapor, rain, snow, sleet, and hail. Finally, our class learned to classify clouds and tell how they form.

Your child has learned many new vocabulary words to talk about water in our environment. Help your child to make these words a part of his or her own vocabulary by using them when you talk together about water.

salinity
aquifer
water table
reservoir
condensation
evaporation
precipitation
sublimation
sleet

The following pages include activities that you and your child can do together. By participating in your child's education, you will help to bring the learning home.

Family Science Activity

Cloud in a Bottle

Materials:

- 2-liter soda bottle
- warm water
- match

Steps

1. Pour about 1/3 cup of warm water into the bottle.
2. Light a match and let it burn briefly. Then blow it out and drop it into the bottle. Let the smoke fill the bottle. The smoke will seem to disappear in a few seconds. Screw the cap on the bottle.
3. Give the bottle a hard squeeze about 10 times. Then squeeze the bottle again and hold the pressure for a few seconds. As soon as you quickly release the squeeze. As soon as you release the squeeze, you'll see some fog form inside the bottle. The fog is a cloud!

Talk About It

Clouds form when water vapor changes into droplets or crystals. Air pressure is part of the process. Squeezing the bottle increases the air pressure. When you release the pressure, the air expands and becomes cooler. The cooling process helps vapor form into droplets. The smoke helps because water vapor forms drops more easily when there are particles in the air.

Workbook

Vocabulary Practice

Water on Earth

Write a vocabulary word to complete each sentence.

1. Snow, sleet, and rain are examples of _____.

2. Groundwater can flow in an _____.

3. Water vapor turning into liquid is _____.

4. Frozen rain drops are _____.

5. A lake that forms behind a dam is a _____.

6. Liquid water changing to water vapor is _____.

7. The _____ is the top layer of groundwater in an aquifer.

8. Ice changing into water vapor without first melting is _____.

9. Ocean water has a higher _____ than fresh water.

Ocean True or False

Write T if the sentence is true. Write F if the sentence is false. Change each false sentence to make it true.

Ex. Oceans cover about 25% of Earth. __F__
  75%

1. Drinking water can come from the ocean. ___

2. The Atlantic Ocean is the deepest ocean. ___

3. Ocean water is saltier in some places than in others. ___

4. The Indian Ocean is the largest ocean. ___

5. There are five oceans in the hydrosphere. ___

6. Much of the salt we add to our food comes from the ocean. ___

Fun Fact

Did you know that most of our rainwater comes from the oceans? Up to 79 inches of water evaporates from the Pacific and Indian Oceans alone!

Name _____

Write what you think the following vocabulary words mean in the spaces below.

Anemometer _____

Barometer _____

Rain gauge _____

Climate _____

Convection current _____

Air mass _____

Front _____

After you have read the chapter and understand the definitions of the words, choose the correct vocabulary terms from above to fill in the following blanks.

1. When two air masses of different temperatures come together, they can cause a(n) _____.

2. The precipitation, average temperatures, and temperature changes in an area make up the _____ of that area.

3. The device used to measure the amount of air pressure needed to move a dial or mercury is called a(n) _____.

4. When air stays in one area for a period of time, it is called a(n) _____.

5. When a line of clouds moves across the sky, it is an example of a(n) _____.

6. The device with cups that spin as the wind speed changes is called a(n) _____.

7. The cylinder-shaped device with a ruler on the side that measures rain is called a(n) _____.

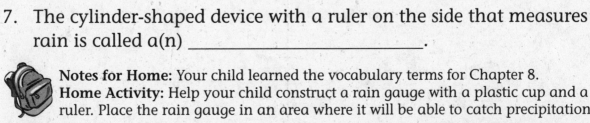

Notes for Home: Your child learned the vocabulary terms for Chapter 8.
Home Activity: Help your child construct a rain gauge with a plastic cup and a ruler. Place the rain gauge in an area where it will be able to catch precipitation.

Draw Conclusions

A meteorologist has made the following observations about the weather outside:

Observations About the Weather

Winds have picked up to high speeds.
Vertical clouds have grown in size.
Precipitation, in the form of water droplets, has begun to fall heavily.
Precipitation, in the form of hail, has begun to fall.

Apply It!

Use the graphic organizer on page 75 to draw a conclusion about what type of weather phenomenon is occurring in the example. List the facts from the meteorologist's observation chart and draw an appropriate conclusion in the boxes provided.

Name _____

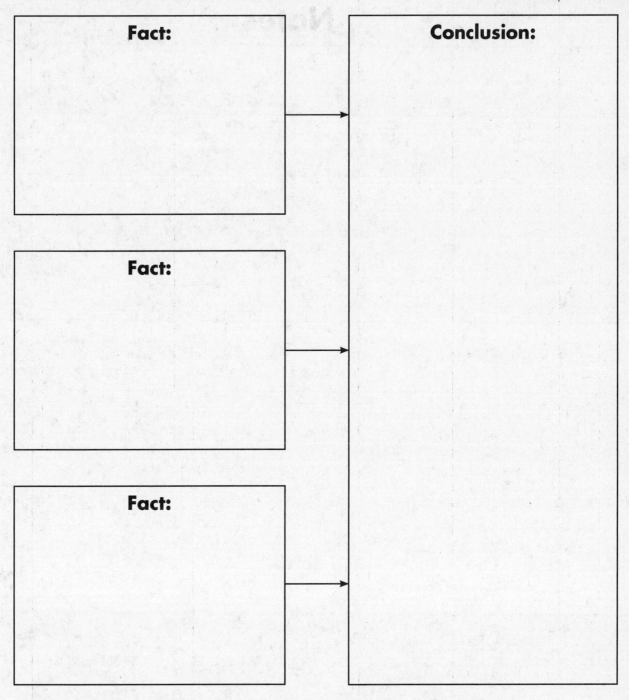

Fact:

Fact:

Fact:

Conclusion:

Notes for Home: Your child learned how to draw conclusions.
Home Activity: Discuss with your child what the weather conditions might be like tomorrow. Help your child draw a conclusion about the weather.

Notes

Name _____

Lesson 1: How does air move?

Before You Read Lesson 1

Read each statement below. Place a check mark in the circle to indicate whether you agree or disagree with the statement.

	Agree	Disagree
1. Air pressure increases as you get farther away from the ground.	○	○
2. There are five layers in Earth's atmosphere.	○	○
3. Convection currents can cause patterns of clouds and precipitation.	○	○
4. Jet streams are slow winds that are found near Earth's surface.	○	○

After You Read Lesson 1

Reread each statement above. If the lesson supports your choice, place a check mark in the *Correct* circle. Then explain how the text supports your choice. If the lesson does not support your choice, place a check mark in the *Incorrect* circle. Then explain why your choice is wrong.

	Correct	Incorrect
1. _____	○	○
_____		
2. _____	○	○
_____		
3. _____	○	○
_____		
4. _____	○	○
_____		

Notes for Home: Your child has completed a pre/post inventory of key concepts in the lesson.
Home Activity: Have your child explain to you how pressure and temperature change as one moves higher into the atmosphere.

Reviewing Terms: Sentence Completion

Complete each sentence with the correct term.

_____ 1. In a _____, gases or liquids rise and sink in a circular path. (jet stream, convection current)

_____ 2. A band of very fast wind that is formed by the different temperatures between huge convection currents is called a _____. (convection current, jet stream)

Reviewing Main Ideas: True or False

Write **T** (True) or **F** (False) on the line before each statement.

_____ 3. There are five layers of Earth's atmosphere.

_____ 4. Most weather conditions occur only in the troposphere.

_____ 5. Air pressure increases as you go up in altitude because gas particles in the air get farther apart.

_____ 6. Wind occurs as air moves from a place of low air pressure to a place of high air pressure.

_____ 7. When two kinds of air are next to each other, the cooler air will sink and force the warmer air to rise.

_____ 8. The combination of the movement of huge convection currents and the spinning of Earth causes regional wind patterns.

Applying Strategies: Calculate

9. If you have 3 liters of air in your lungs and $\frac{2}{10}$ of that is oxygen, how many milliliters of oxygen are in your lungs? Explain how you arrived at your answer. (2 points)

Name _____

Lesson 2: What are air masses?

Before You Read Lesson 2

Read each statement below. Place a check mark in the circle to indicate whether you agree or disagree with the statement.

		Agree	Disagree
1.	The air that forms an air mass has different properties throughout it.	○	○
2.	Air masses help to determine the weather in an area.	○	○
3.	Fronts occur within an air mass.	○	○
4.	Warm fronts carry warm air.	○	○

After You Read Lesson 2

Reread each statement above. If the lesson supports your choice, place a check mark in the *Correct* circle. Then explain how the text supports your choice. If the lesson does not support your choice, place a check mark in the *Incorrect* circle. Then explain why your choice is wrong.

		Correct	Incorrect
1.	_____	○	○
	_____		
2.	_____	○	○
	_____		
3.	_____	○	○
	_____		
4.	_____	○	○
	_____		

Notes for Home: Your child has completed a pre/post inventory of key concepts in the lesson.
Home Activity: Have your child create a chart that compares the four basic types of air masses.

Reviewing Terms: Matching

Match each definition with the correct term.

_____ 1. a boundary between two air masses   **a.** air mass

_____ 2. a large body of air with similar   **b.** front
properties throughout

Reviewing Concepts: Sentence Completion

Complete each sentence with the correct word.

_____ 3. The most important properties of an air mass are its
_____ and amount of water vapor. (temperature,
pressure)

_____ 4. Air masses move because of _____. (rain, winds)

_____ 5. A maritime tropical air mass is warm and _____.
(dry, humid)

_____ 6. A _____ front moves back and forth over the same
area. (warm, stationary)

_____ 7. At _____ fronts, warmer air gradually rises above
cooler air. (warm, cold)

_____ 8. Heavy precipitation often falls at a _____ front.
(warm, cold)

Applying Strategies: Summarize

Use complete sentences to answer question 9. (2 points)
9. Summarize the way that cold fronts differ from warm fronts.

_____

_____

_____

Name _____

Lesson 3: What causes severe weather?

Before You Read Lesson 3

Read each statement below. Place a check mark in the circle to indicate whether you agree or disagree with the statement.

		Agree	Disagree
1.	Typically, air currents are downward during the final stage in a thunderstorm.	○	○
2.	You will be safe from lightning if you stand under a tree.	○	○
3.	When a spinning column of air touches the ground, it is called a tornado.	○	○
4.	Tornadoes are always more destructive than hurricanes.	○	○

After You Read Lesson 3

Reread each statement above. If the lesson supports your choice, place a check mark in the *Correct* circle. Then explain how the text supports your choice. If the lesson does not support your choice, place a check mark in the *Incorrect* circle. Then explain why your choice is wrong.

	Correct	Incorrect
1. _____	○	○
_____		
2. _____	○	○
_____		
3. _____	○	○
_____		
4. _____	○	○
_____		

Notes for Home: Your child has completed a pre/post inventory of key concepts in the lesson.
Home Activity: Discuss with your child what types of severe weather your community experiences. Review the ways you and your child can prepare for such occurrences.

Name _____

Reviewing Terms: Matching

Match each description with the correct term. Write the letter of the term on the line next to the description.

_____ 1. a funnel cloud that touches the ground

_____ 2. a storm that often starts with strong, quickly rising currents of moist air

_____ 3. a huge electrical spark moving between areas of opposite charge

_____ 4. storms that get their energy from warm ocean water

a. thunderstorm
b. lightning
c. tornado
d. hurricane

Reviewing Concepts: True or False

Write **T** (True) or **F** (False) on the line before each statement.

_____ 5. A severe storm warning means that severe thunderstorms have formed and people should get inside.

_____ 6. Different areas of a thunderstorm cloud have positive and negative electrical charges.

_____ 7. Hurricanes usually only last a few minutes.

_____ 8. When water vapor from the ocean condenses, it releases energy that can build into a hurricane.

Applying Strategies: Sequence

Use complete sentences to answer question 9. (2 points)

9. Sequence the stages of the formation of a thunderstorm.

_____

_____

_____

_____

_____

© Pearson Education, Inc.

Lesson 4: How are weather forecasts made?

Before You Read Lesson 4

Read each statement below. Place a check mark in the circle to indicate whether you agree or disagree with the statement.

	Agree	Disagree
1. A barometer uses spinning cups to measure wind speed.	○	○
2. Hygrometers are used to find out the amount of moisture in the air.	○	○
3. Forecasters look for patterns of weather change to predict future weather.	○	○
4. Fronts occur in areas of high pressure.	○	○

After You Read Lesson 4

Reread each statement above. If the lesson supports your choice, place a check mark in the *Correct* circle. Then explain how the text supports your choice. If the lesson does not support your choice, place a check mark in the *Incorrect* circle. Then explain why your choice is wrong.

	Correct	Incorrect
1. _____	○	○
_____		
2. _____	○	○
_____		
3. _____	○	○
_____		
4. _____	○	○
_____		

Notes for Home: Your child has completed a pre/post inventory of key concepts in the lesson.
Home Activity: With your child, look at the weather page in a newspaper or watch a weather segment on television. Try to identify the symbols used in the forecasts.

Reviewing Terms: Matching

Match each description with the correct term. Write the letter of the term on the line next to the description.

_____ 1. measures the moisture in the air   **a.** anemometer

_____ 2. measures how much rain has fallen   **b.** barometer

_____ 3. shows air pressure   **c.** hygrometer

_____ 4. measures wind speed   **d.** radar

_____ 5. measures winds and precipitation   **e.** rain gauge
         within a storm

Reviewing Concepts: True or False

Write **T** (True) or **F** (False) on the line before each statement.

_____ 6. Returning radar energy can show direction and speed of raindrops.

_____ 7. Forecasters make predictions based on information about past weather conditions.

_____ 8. In the United States, fronts generally move from east to west.

Writing

Use complete sentences to answer question 9. (2 points)

9. Suppose that you are a television weather forecaster in your town. Write a short script describing tomorrow's weather for your town.

_____

_____

_____

_____

Name _____

Lesson 5: What is climate?

Before You Read Lesson 5

Read each statement below. Place a check mark in the circle to indicate whether you agree or disagree with the statement.

	Agree	Disagree
1. Usually climates change faster than daily weather patterns.	○	○
2. Ocean temperatures cool down and heat up faster than air temperatures.	○	○
3. North America's climate was wetter and colder in the 1600s than it is now.	○	○
4. Fossils help scientists understand climate changes long ago.	○	○

After You Read Lesson 5

Reread each statement above. If the lesson supports your choice, place a check mark in the *Correct* circle. Then explain how the text supports your choice. If the lesson does not support your choice, place a check mark in the *Incorrect* circle. Then explain why your choice is wrong.

	Correct	Incorrect
1. _____	○	○
2. _____	○	○
3. _____	○	○
4. _____	○	○

Notes for Home: Your child has completed a pre/post inventory of key concepts in the lesson.
Home Activity: Discuss with your child the climate of your area. What are the average temperatures and amount of precipitation for your area?

Reviewing Terms: Matching

Match the definition with the correct term. Write the letter of the term on the line next to the definition.

_____ 1. the average of weather conditions over a long time

_____ 2. all the conditions in one place at a single moment

a. weather

b. climate

Reviewing Concepts: Sentence Completion

Complete each sentence with the correct word or phrase.

_____ 3. Climates _____ change much on a daily basis. (do, do not)

_____ 4. Oceans affect climates by _____ the rise and fall of air temperatures. (slowing, speeding up)

_____ 5. A rain shadow is the side of a mountain that _____ clouds or rain. (has, does not have)

_____ 6. The Gulf Stream _____ the winds above it. (warms, cools)

_____ 7. Volcanic eruptions and asteroid impacts may have brought about _____ climates in the distant past. (warmer, cooler)

_____ 8. Scientists _____ on why climates change. (agree, disagree)

Applying Strategies: Draw Conclusions

Use complete sentences to answer question 9. (2 points)

9. How have scientists been able to describe past climates?

_____

_____

_____

_____

Typhoons

Typhoons, more commonly known as hurricanes in the United States, have been studied for many years. The bar graph below lists by month the number of typhoons that have occurred in the Bay of Bengal region in the years 1945–2000. Use this bar graph to answer the questions.

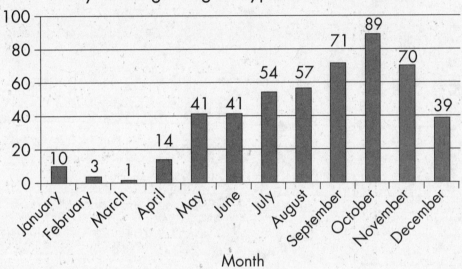

Bay of Bengal Region Typhoons 1945–2000

1. Which month has the least number of typhoons?

   _____

2. Which month has the greatest number of typhoons?

   _____

3. How many more typhoons occurred in January than in March?

   _____

4. How many more typhoons occurred in June than in April?

   _____

5. From February to October by how much did the number of typhoons change?

   _____

Notes for Home: Your child has learned how to read a bar graph.
Home Activity: Help your child make a bar graph that shows the frequency of certain daily activities, such as sleeping and eating, during a single week.

Notes

Dear Family,

Our class is studying weather patterns. In the science chapter Weather Patterns, your child has learned what causes air currents and how different kinds of air masses create weather. We have studied how severe weather like storms, tornadoes, and hurricanes form. We have also explored how weather forecasts are made and the differences between climate and weather.

Your child has learned many new vocabulary words that describe weather patterns. Help your child to make these words a part of his or her own vocabulary by using them when you talk together about the weather outside.

> convection current
> air mass
> front
> barometer
> anemometer
> rain gauge
> climate

The following pages include activities that you and your child can do together. By participating in your child's education, you will help to bring the learning home.

© Pearson Education, Inc.

Family Science Activity
Weather Check

Use this chart to follow the weather forecasts for five days. You could also compare the accuracy of two different forecasts, such as one on television and one in a newspaper.

	Predicted Weather	Actual Weather
Day 1	High temperature: Low temperature: Weather conditions:	High temperature: Low temperature: Weather conditions:
Day 2	High temperature: Low temperature: Weather conditions:	High temperature: Low temperature: Weather conditions:
Day 3	High temperature: Low temperature: Weather conditions:	High temperature: Low temperature: Weather conditions:
Day 4	High temperature: Low temperature: Weather conditions:	High temperature: Low temperature: Weather conditions:
Day 5	High temperature: Low temperature: Weather conditions:	High temperature: Low temperature: Weather conditions:

Talk About It

On which day was the forecast most accurate?
What kinds of weather do you think are hardest to predict accurately?
Which is probably more accurate: a prediction about the weather tomorrow or next week? Why?

Weather Matching

Draw a line from the term to its definition.

air mass   all the outside conditions in one place at a single moment

convection current   a boundary between two air masses

front   a tool that shows air pressure

anemometer   a tool that measures wind speed

barometer   the average of weather conditions over a long time

weather   a large body of air with similar properties

climate   occurs when gases or liquids rise and sink in a circular path

Fun Fact

Air has weight. Air pressure changes when air becomes heavier or lighter. The average weight of air is about 15 pounds on every square inch of your body.

© Pearson Education, Inc.

Weather Patterns

Complete this weather report using chapter vocabulary words.

rain gauge   barometer   convection current
air mass   anemometer   front

Hello, this is your WWET reporter, speaking to you live. Right now we have a lovely day thanks to the warm tropical _____ above us. The gentle beeze is being created by a _____. My _____ shows that the wind speed right now is quite low. But hold tight! My _____ measurements have dropped dramatically in the last hour. That means the air pressure is dropping, and that means trouble. We've got a huge cold _____ approaching from the northwest. Right now it's over Neartown, where the _____ shows they've already received 4 inches of rain.

The words in the box are vocabulary terms from Chapter 9. Use your textbook to look up the definitions of the terms. Then, fill in the blanks below with the vocabulary term that you think best fits the sentence.

> crust   mantle   core   plates   **mechanical weathering**
> **chemical weathering   igneous   sedimentary   metamorphic**

1. Gneiss and slate are _____ rocks.

2. Temperatures can be as hot as 5000°C in the _____ of Earth.

3. The movement of _____ can form mountains and valleys.

4. When water freezes in the cracks of rocks and expands, _____ has occurred.

5. The thickest section of Earth is called the _____.

6. Gravel, sandstone, and conglomerate are all types of _____ rocks.

7. The topmost layer of Earth is the _____.

8. When rain soaks away rock below the ground to form caves, _____ has occurred.

9. Basalt, pumice, and granite are _____ rocks.

Notes for Home: Your child learned the vocabulary terms for Chapter 9.
Home Activity: Have your child use the vocabulary terms to explain the difference between igneous, sedimentary, and metamorphic rocks.

Summarize

Read the newspaper article.

Mount Vesuvius

Mount Vesuvius, located in southern Italy, is a composite volcano. This type of volcano is made up of alternate layers of ash and lava. A major eruption happened on August 24, A.D. 79. This eruption spewed tons of molten ash, pumice, and sulfuric gas miles into the atmosphere. About 2,000 people were killed in the cities of Herculaneum and Pompeii.

Apply It!

Use the graphic organizer on page 87 to summarize the information in the science article. Place the details in the smaller boxes and write a summary in the large box.

Name _____

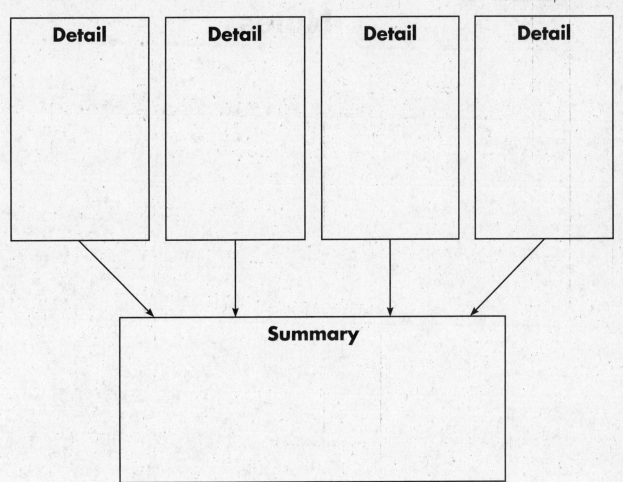

Detail	Detail	Detail	Detail

Summary

Notes for Home: Your child learned how to summarize scientific information.
Home Activity: Read a short article in a newspaper or magazine with your child.
Have your child give you a summary of the article.

Notes

Lesson 1: What is the structure of Earth?

Before You Read Lesson 1

Read each statement below. Place a check mark in the circle to indicate whether you agree or disagree with the statement.

	Agree	Disagree
1. Earth is made up of several layers.	○	○
2. The crust is the outermost layer of Earth.	○	○
3. Temperatures are generally higher in the mantle than in the core.	○	○
4. Scientists are able to go into the mantle and core to learn about them.	○	○

After You Read Lesson 1

Reread each statement above. If the lesson supports your choice, place a check mark in the *Correct* circle. Then explain how the text supports your choice. If the lesson does not support your choice, place a check mark in the *Incorrect* circle. Then explain why your choice is wrong.

	Correct	Incorrect
1. _____	○	○
_____		
2. _____	○	○
_____		
3. _____	○	○
_____		
4. _____	○	○
_____		

Notes for Home: Your child has completed a pre/post inventory of key concepts in the lesson.
Home Activity: Have your child draw a diagram of Earth and label the different layers correctly.

Reviewing Terms: Matching

Match each definition with the correct term. Write the letter on the line next to the definition.

_____ 1. the very center of Earth; made mostly of iron

_____ 2. the outermost and thinnest of Earth's layers

_____ 3. between the crust and the core; makes up most of Earth's material

_____ 4. an instrument that records earthquake waves

a. mantle

b. core

c. seismograph

d. crust

Reviewing Concepts: Sentence Completion

Complete each sentence with the correct word.

_____ 5. _____ crust is made mostly of basalt and is about 6 to 11 kilometers thick. (Continental, Oceanic)

_____ 6. The oceanic crust begins at the continental _____. (shelf, rise)

_____ 7. The top part of the mantle and the crust above it form the _____. (hydrosphere, lithosphere)

_____ 8. Liquid in the _____ core flows in currents. (inner, outer)

Writing

Use complete sentences to answer question 9. (2 points)

9. Describe three ways that scientists study Earth's layers.

_____

_____

_____

_____

_____

Lesson 2: What causes earthquakes and volcanoes?

Before You Read Lesson 2

Read each statement below. Place a check mark in the circle to indicate whether you agree or disagree with the statement.

	Agree	Disagree
1. Mountains are formed by the movement of Earth's plates.	○	○
2. Plates move very quickly.	○	○
3. Earthquakes occur at faults, or cracks in the crust of Earth.	○	○
4. Volcanoes can only form on land.	○	○

After You Read Lesson 2

Reread each statement above. If the lesson supports your choice, place a check mark in the *Correct* circle. Then explain how the text supports your choice. If the lesson does not support your choice, place a check mark in the *Incorrect* circle. Then explain why your choice is wrong.

	Correct	Incorrect
1. _____	○	○
2. _____	○	○
3. _____	○	○
4. _____	○	○

 Notes for Home: Your child has completed a pre/post inventory of key concepts in the lesson.
Home Activity: Have your child explain to you why plates move and what land features plates form when they meet each other.

Reviewing Terms: Sentence Completion

Complete each sentence with the correct term.

_____ 1. A _____ is a section of the lithosphere. (focus, plate)

_____ 2. Cracks in Earth's crust where surrounding rock has moved or shifted are called _____. (faults, plates)

Reviewing Concepts: True or False

Write **T** (True) or **F** (False) on the line before each statement.

_____ 3. Plates move because of gravity and convection currents.

_____ 4. The Atlantic Ocean is the site of a spreading plate boundary.

_____ 5. Earthquakes most often occur at faults that are away from plate boundaries.

_____ 6. Energy released in an earthquake can cause landslides and tsunamis.

_____ 7. Most volcanoes form near colliding plate boundaries.

_____ 8. A mountain forms when a volcano reaches the surface of the water in an ocean.

Applying Strategies: Summarize

Construct a table to answer question 9. (2 points)

9. Construct a table that summarizes information about three kinds of plate boundaries.

© Pearson Education, Inc.

Lesson 3: What is weathering?

Before You Read Lesson 3

Read each statement below. Place a check mark in the circle to indicate whether you agree or disagree with the statement.

	Agree	Disagree
1. Weathering is an explosive force that blows rocks apart.	O	O
2. Gravity and ice can cause mechanical weathering.	O	O
3. Chemical weathering occurs faster in deserts than in rainforests.	O	O
4. Weathering helps to make the mixture of sediments that make up soil.	O	O

After You Read Lesson 3

Reread each statement above. If the lesson supports your choice, place a check mark in the *Correct* circle. Then explain how the text supports your choice. If the lesson does not support your choice, place a check mark in the *Incorrect* circle. Then explain why your choice is wrong.

	Correct	Incorrect
1. _____ _____	O	O
2. _____ _____	O	O
3. _____ _____	O	O
4. _____ _____	O	O

Notes for Home: Your child has completed a pre/post inventory of key concepts in the lesson.
Home Activity: Have your child compare and contrast mechanical and chemical weathering using a Venn diagram.

Reviewing Terms: Matching

Match each definition or example with the correct term. Write the letter on the line next to the definition or example.

_____ 1. the formation of caves

_____ 2. breaking of rock into smaller pieces by gravity or other forces

_____ 3. ice wedging

_____ 4. changes in rocks by chemical processes

a. chemical weathering

b. mechanical weathering

Reviewing Concepts: True or False

Write **T** (True) or **F** (False) on the line before each statement.

_____ 5. The rate of mechanical weathering depends on the materials in a rock and the conditions around it.

_____ 6. Areas with little rain will have a lot of chemical weathering.

_____ 7. Soil is a mixture of sediments from weathered rock, decayed materials, gases from air, and water.

_____ 8. Bedrock can eventually become soil sediment.

Applying Strategies: Calculating

Show all work when answering question 9. (2 points)

9. In a wheelbarrow, you have 2 kilograms of soil for your garden. If 8 percent of it is organic matter (decayed materials from organisms), how many grams of organic matter do you have?

Name _____

Lesson 4: What is erosion?

Before You Read Lesson 4

Read each statement below. Place a check mark in the circle to indicate whether you agree or disagree with the statement.

	Agree	Disagree
1. The processes of erosion and deposition are the same.	◯	◯
2. Ocean waves cause erosion on beaches.	◯	◯
3. Wind can cause both erosion and weathering.	◯	◯
4. Wind erosion only occurs in deserts.	◯	◯

After You Read Lesson 4

Reread each statement above. If the lesson supports your choice, place a check mark in the *Correct* circle. Then explain how the text supports your choice. If the lesson does not support your choice, place a check mark in the *Incorrect* circle. Then explain why your choice is wrong.

	Correct	Incorrect
1. _____ _____	◯	◯
2. _____ _____	◯	◯
3. _____ _____	◯	◯
4. _____ _____	◯	◯

Notes for Home: Your child has completed a pre/post inventory of key concepts in the lesson.
Home Activity: Have your child demonstrate the process of erosion by slowly pouring a cup of water on a mound of dirt outside. Ask your child to explain what changes have occurred.

Reviewing Terms: Matching

Match each definition with the correct term. Write the letter on the line next to the definition.

_____ 1. placing of materials in a new place

_____ 2. movement of materials away from one place

_____ 3. a place where heavy sediments are deposited when a river meets an ocean

a. delta

b. deposition

c. erosion

Reviewing Concepts: Sentence Completion

Complete each sentence with the correct word or phrase.

_____ 4. In a landslide, _____ quickly pulls rocks and dirt downhill. (gravity, wind)

_____ 5. _____ rivers carry more sediments. (Fast, Slow)

_____ 6. Rocks are ground to sediment under moving _____. (glaciers, icebergs)

_____ 7. The constant action of _____ is a major source of erosion along shorelines. (waves, wind)

_____ 8. Large, loose deposits of sand are called _____. (deltas, sand dunes)

Applying Strategies: Cause and Effect

Use complete sentences to answer question 9. (2 points)

9. What can cause a sand dune to slowly move in the direction of the wind?

_____

_____

_____

_____

Name _____

Lesson 5: How are minerals identified?

Before You Read Lesson 5

Read each statement below. Place a check mark in the circle to indicate whether you agree or disagree with the statement.

	Agree	Disagree
1. You can find minerals in the rocks and soil of Earth.	○	○
2. All minerals have the same level of hardness.	○	○
3. You can classify minerals by how shiny they look.	○	○
4. Scientists have already identified every mineral that exists on Earth.	○	○

After You Read Lesson 5

Reread each statement above. If the lesson supports your choice, place a check mark in the *Correct* circle. Then explain how the text supports your choice. If the lesson does not support your choice, place a check mark in the *Incorrect* circle. Then explain why your choice is wrong.

	Correct	Incorrect
1. _____	○	○
_____		
2. _____	○	○
_____		
3. _____	○	○
_____		
4. _____	○	○
_____		

Notes for Home: Your child has completed a pre/post inventory of key concepts in the lesson.
Home Activity: Discuss with your child what common types of minerals people need for good health.

Name _____

Reviewing Concepts: Sentence Completion

Complete each sentence with the correct term.

_____ 1. A mineral's _____ will cause it to break in definite patterns. (texture, shape)

_____ 2. A mineral's _____ is the way light is reflected by its surface. (hardness, luster)

_____ 3. Some minerals can be identified by their _____. (smell, size)

_____ 4. A(n) _____ is a naturally made solid that has a regular arrangement of particles in it. (acid, mineral)

_____ 5. The _____ is used to determine the hardness of a mineral. (luster, Mohs scale)

_____ 6. *Gritty*, *smooth*, *sticky*, and *powdery* all describe a mineral's _____. (smell, texture)

_____ 7. The color of a mineral in its powdered form is called its _____. (texture, streak)

_____ 8. Minerals can be found in soil and in _____. (acids, rocks)

Applying Strategies: Draw Conclusions

Use complete sentences to answer question 9. (2 points)

9. How do scientists identify unknown minerals? How would a scientist tell the difference between calcite and quartz?

_____

_____

_____

_____

_____

_____

© Pearson Education, Inc.

Workbook

Lesson 6: How are rocks classified?

Before You Read Lesson 6

Read each statement below. Place a check mark in the circle to indicate whether you agree or disagree with the statement.

	Agree	Disagree
1. In general, all rocks are formed in the same way.	○	○
2. Igneous rock is formed by pressing layers of rock together.	○	○
3. Many fossils can be found in sedimentary rock.	○	○
4. Rocks can change from one type of rock to another, or not change at all.	○	○

After You Read Lesson 6

Reread each statement above. If the lesson supports your choice, place a check mark in the *Correct* circle. Then explain how the text supports your choice. If the lesson does not support your choice, place a check mark in the *Incorrect* circle. Then explain why your choice is wrong.

	Correct	Incorrect
1. _____ _____	○	○
2. _____ _____	○	○
3. _____ _____	○	○
4. _____ _____	○	○

Notes for Home: Your child has completed a pre/post inventory of key concepts in the lesson.
Home Activity: With a common food item, like chocolate chips, demonstrate with your child how the processes of melting, cooling, and pressure change the form of the original item.

Name _____

Reviewing Terms: Matching

Match each description with the correct term. Write the letter on the line next to the description.

_____ 1. rocks that form when layers of materials settle on top of each other and harden

_____ 2. type of rock formed when existing rock is squeezed and heated at very high temperatures

_____ 3. rocks that form when melted rock cools and hardens

a. igneous

b. sedimentary

c. metamorphic

Reviewing Concepts: True or False

Write **T** (True) or **F** (False) on the line before each statement.

_____ 4. Melted rock that cools quickly results in igneous rock with large mineral crystals.

_____ 5. Pumice is a rock that has many tiny holes where gases were trapped.

_____ 6. Plant and animal fossils are most often found in metamorphic rock.

_____ 7. Rocks cannot change from one kind to another.

_____ 8. Over time, rock layers can be bent and turned over by processes such as volcanic eruptions.

Writing

Use complete sentences to answer question 9. (2 points)

9. A scientist finds a rock with fossils at two different levels. Tell why he or she might conclude that the fossils on the bottom are older than the fossils at the top.

_____

_____

_____

© Pearson Education, Inc.

Classifying Solid Figures

Many minerals are used as birthstones. Below is a list of the first six months and their birthstones. Use the information from the list and from the chapter to answer the following questions.

MONTH	BIRTHSTONE
January	Garnet
February	Amethyst
March	Aquamarine
April	Diamond
May	Emerald
June	Pearl

1. This is a picture of April's birthstone. What shapes do you see in the picture?

   _____

   _____

2. This is February's birthstone. What shapes do you see?

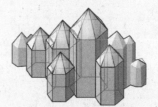

   _____

   _____

3. This is a garnet crystal. What kind(s) of shapes do you see?

   _____

   _____

Notes for Home: Your child has learned about how to recognize minerals by their shapes.
Home Activity: Help your child figure out the appropriate birthstones for every member of the family. Have your child draw the shapes of what they think the crystals will look like.

Notes

Dear Family,

Your child is learning about how Earth changes. In the science chapter Earth's Changing Surface, we have studied Earth's structure, including the crust, mantle, and core. We have learned about constructive and destructive forces that change Earth's surface. We have studied rapid changes, like earthquakes and volcanoes, and gradual changes, like shifting plates, weather, erosion, and deposition. Finally, we have learned how scientists classify minerals and rocks.

Your child has learned many new vocabulary words that describe structures, forces, and objects on Earth. Help your child to make these words a part of his or her own vocabulary by using them when you talk together about Earth's features.

crust
mantle
core
plate
mechanical weathering
chemical weathering
igneous
sedimentary
metamorphic

The following pages include activities that you and your child can do together. By participating in your child's education, you will help to bring the learning home.

Family Science Activity

Rock Hunt

Collect and classify rocks and minerals with your family. Use these charts to classify samples you find during family walks or hikes. Consider the properties to describe rocks. Then use the categories to classify them.

	Rock 1	Rock 2	Rock 3
hardness			
luster (the way it reflects light)			
color			
streak (the kind of mark it makes)			

	Rock 1	Rock 2	Rock 3
Description			
Classification: igneous, sedimentary, or metamorphic?			

Talk About It

All rocks are made up of minerals. Which rocks are made of more than one mineral? How can you tell? Choose one rock. Describe how it might have been formed. Then tell how it might change in the rock cycle.

Vocabulary Practice
Earth's Changing Surface

Fill in the missing letters to complete the words.

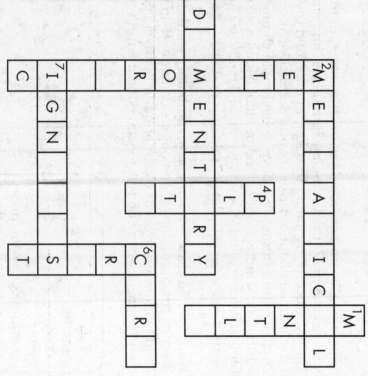

Look at this picture of an active volcano.
Label the different parts of the volcano using the words in the box.

lava flowing down
steep side of the volcano
main vent or crater
lava flows from a small vent

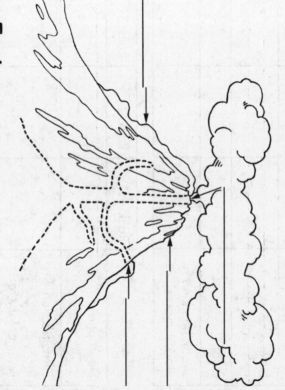

Fun Fact
Chances are good that somewhere in the world there are 20 volcanoes erupting right now!

Fill out the following feature Analysis Grid. The words listed on the side of the chart are the vocabulary terms for the chapter. Write a "+" sign in the box if you think the word on the top of the chart is a good example of the vocabulary term or relates to its meaning. Write a "−" sign if you think it is not a good example or does not relate to the meaning of the term.

	Wood	Oil	Coal	Water	Sun	Electricity	Garbage
Geothermal Energy							
Renewable Resources							
Nonrenewable Resources							
Hydroelectric Energy							
Fossil Fuel Energy							
Solar Energy							
Biomass Energy							

© Pearson Education, Inc.

Notes for Home: Your child learned the vocabulary terms for Chapter 10.
Home Activity: Help your child pronounce, spell, and define the vocabulary terms correctly.

TARGET SKILL ◎ Main Idea and Details

Read the science article.

Oil Spills

Oil spills are dangerous to the environment and take a lot of work to clean up. During an oil spill in the Gulf of Alaska, about 11 million gallons of oil spilled into the water. This oil killed millions of animals including birds, otters, and even whales. It took thousands of people to help clean up all of the oil. Workers had to clean not only the beaches but animals as well.

Apply It!

Use the graphic organizer on page 99 to list the main idea and the important details from the article.

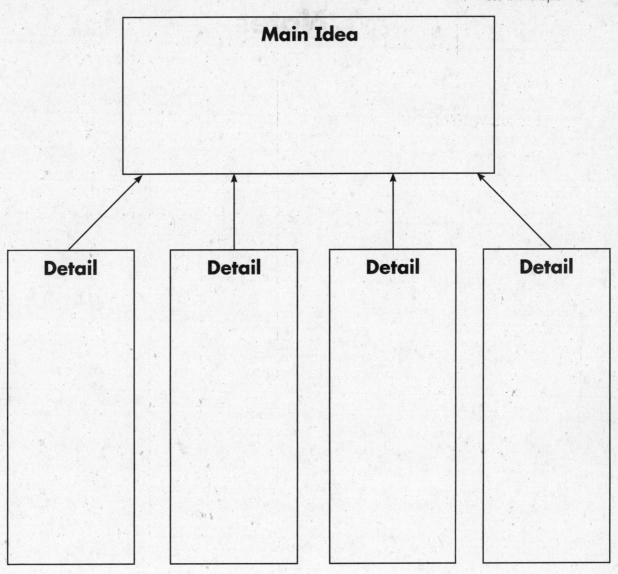

Main Idea

Detail

Detail

Detail

Detail

© Pearson Education, Inc.

Notes for Home: Your child learned how to identify the main idea and supporting details in an article.
Home Activity: With your child read a short passage in a book or magazine. Have your child pick out the main idea and details from the passage.

Notes

Lesson 1: What are nonrenewable energy resources?

Before You Read Lesson 1

Read each statement below. Place a check mark in the circle to indicate whether you agree or disagree with the statement.

		Agree	Disagree
1.	A renewable resource is one that cannot be replaced.	○	○
2.	Fossil fuels are used to produce energy.	○	○
3.	Natural gas supplies us with gasoline and diesel fuel.	○	○
4.	When oil and coal are burned, toxins are released into the air.	○	○

After You Read Lesson 1

Reread each statement above. If the lesson supports your choice, place a check mark in the *Correct* circle. Then explain how the text supports your choice. If the lesson does not support your choice, place a check mark in the *Incorrect* circle. Then explain why your choice is wrong.

		Correct	Incorrect
1.	_____	○	○
2.	_____	○	○
3.	_____	○	○
4.	_____	○	○

Notes for Home: Your child has completed a pre/post inventory of key concepts in the lesson.
Home Activity: Brainstorm with your child about types of renewable and nonrenewable resources.

Reviewing Terms: Matching

Match each definition with the correct term. Write the letter on the line next to the definition.

_____ 1. a resource that cannot be replaced as fast as it is used

_____ 2. energy source formed from things that lived long ago

_____ 3. a resource that can be replaced in a reasonable amount of time

_____ 4. any supply that will meet a need for materials or energy

a. resource

b. renewable resource

c. nonrenewable resource

d. fossil fuel

Reviewing Concepts: True or False

Write **T** (True) or **F** (False) on the line before each statement.

_____ 5. Coal is a renewable resource that forms from plants.

_____ 6. Coal fuels most electric power plants.

_____ 7. Natural gas is often found where crude oil is found.

_____ 8. It is easier to get large amounts of energy from fossil fuels than from other energy sources.

Applying Strategies: Main Idea and Details

Use complete sentences to answer question 9. (2 points)

9. Read the following paragraph. Tell what the main idea is and identify two details.

Coal is an important source of heat energy. When coal burns, it releases energy that began long ago when sunlight shone on plant leaves. Today, coal fuels most electric power plants in the country.

_____

_____

_____

Lesson 2: What are other energy resources?

Before You Read Lesson 2

Read each statement below. Place a check mark in the circle to indicate whether you agree or disagree with the statement.

	Agree	Disagree
1. Energy from sunlight can be used for heat and electricity.	○	○
2. The power of wind is used to turn turbines and create electricity.	○	○
3. Hydroelectric power plants pollute.	○	○
4. Geothermal energy can make electricity only during the evening hours.	○	○

After You Read Lesson 2

Reread each statement above. If the lesson supports your choice, place a check mark in the *Correct* circle. Then explain how the text supports your choice. If the lesson does not support your choice, place a check mark in the *Incorrect* circle. Then explain why your choice is wrong.

	Correct	Incorrect
1. _____ _____	○	○
2. _____ _____	○	○
3. _____ _____	○	○
4. _____ _____	○	○

Notes for Home: Your child has completed a pre/post inventory of key concepts in the lesson.
Home Activity: Help your child make a chart that lists the advantages and disadvantages of each kind of alternative energy source.

Reviewing Terms: Matching

Match each definition with the correct term. Write the letter on the line next to the definition.

_____ 1. electricity made with the energy of flowing water

_____ 2. energy from sunlight

_____ 3. material that was recently alive, such as grasses or animal wastes

_____ 4. energy produced by heat inside Earth

a. solar energy

b. hydroelectric

c. geothermal

d. biomass

Reviewing Concepts: Sentence Completion

Complete each sentence with the correct word or phrase.

_____ 5. Solar energy systems for making electricity are _____ to make and maintain. (expensive, inexpensive)

_____ 6. Wind turbines spin _____ in light winds than old windmills did. (faster, slower)

_____ 7. Factories were often built near _____ in order to use the energy of flowing water. (lakes, rivers)

_____ 8. Geothermal plants can only be built in places where very hot rocks are _____ Earth's surface. (deep within, close to)

Writing

Use complete sentences to answer question 9. (2 points)

9. Is biomass a renewable or nonrenewable resource? Explain.

_____

_____

_____

_____

Lesson 3: What are other resources?

Before You Read Lesson 3

Read each statement below. Place a check mark in the circle to indicate whether you agree or disagree with the statement.

		Agree	Disagree
1.	Minerals are nonrenewable resources.	○	○
2.	Water, soil, and air are not considered to be resources.	○	○
3.	It takes longer to renew water, soil, and air than it does to renew coal, oil, and minerals.	○	○
4.	Mining and power plants can pollute the air.	○	○

After You Read Lesson 3

Reread each statement above. If the lesson supports your choice, place a check mark in the *Correct* circle. Then explain how the text supports your choice. If the lesson does not support your choice, place a check mark in the *Incorrect* circle. Then explain why your choice is wrong.

		Correct	Incorrect
1.	_____	○	○
	_____		
2.	_____	○	○
	_____		
3.	_____	○	○
	_____		
4.	_____	○	○
	_____		

Notes for Home: Your child has completed a pre/post inventory of key concepts in the lesson.
Home Activity: Discuss ways air and water pollution can affect the life of all living creatures on Earth.

Reviewing Concepts: Sentence Completion

Complete each sentence with the correct word or phrase.

_____ 1. The mineral resources salt and iron are _____ to find. (hard, easy)

_____ 2. Steel is made by mixing iron with _____. (carbon, concrete)

_____ 3. _____ is a resource used to build roads. (Gypsum, Gravel)

_____ 4. All minerals are _____. (renewable, nonrenewable)

_____ 5. Mining companies _____ repairs to land after the mine is used. (make, cannot make)

_____ 6. Water can be recycled through _____. (mining, the water cycle)

_____ 7. Soil is _____ being made from weathering rock and decaying plants. (slowly, quickly)

_____ 8. Water resources can be damaged by pollution or _____. (soil, overuse)

Applying Strategies: Calculating

9. The United States Coast Guard tracks oil spills on all United States waterways. In 2000, there were a total of 8,354 oil spills, 7.8 percent of which were recreational (from boats and water fuel stations). How many fuel spills were recreational? Show your work. (2 points)

Name _____

Lesson 4: Can resources be conserved?

Before You Read Lesson 4

Read each statement below. Place a check mark in the circle to indicate whether you agree or disagree with the statement.

	Agree	Disagree
1. It does not cost very much to clean up pollution.	○	○
2. You can reduce air pollution by using less electricity.	○	○
3. Many everyday items can be reused again and again.	○	○
4. The only purpose of recycling is to save materials.	○	○

After You Read Lesson 4

Reread each statement above. If the lesson supports your choice, place a check mark in the *Correct* circle. Then explain how the text supports your choice. If the lesson does not support your choice, place a check mark in the *Incorrect* circle. Then explain why your choice is wrong.

	Correct	Incorrect
1. _____ _____	○	○
2. _____ _____	○	○
3. _____ _____	○	○
4. _____ _____	○	○

Notes for Home: Your child has completed a pre/post inventory of key concepts in the lesson.
Home Activity: Discuss ways you and your child can conserve resources in your home.

Reviewing Concepts: True or False

Write **T** (True) or **F** (False) on the line before each statement.

_____ 1. The use of machines has had little to do with the development of pollution in air, water, and soil.

_____ 2. It is important to measure the amount of pollution in air, water, and soil.

_____ 3. Conservation laws do little to encourage people to protect natural resources.

_____ 4. Using less electricity contributes to air pollution.

_____ 5. An easy way to save resources is to reuse things.

_____ 6. Recycling means to treat something so that it can be made into something new.

_____ 7. One reason to recycle is to save energy.

_____ 8. It takes more energy to recycle aluminum than it does to get it from a mine.

Applying Strategies: Sequence

Use complete sentences to answer question 9. (2 points)

9. Write the sequence that takes place when plastic is recycled. Use the terms *first, then, next,* and *finally* in your answer.

_____

_____

_____

_____

_____

Name _____

Hydroelectric Energy

The biggest source of renewable energy in the United States comes from hydroelectric power. Hoover Dam alone generates enough electricity to meet the yearly needs of about 1.3 million people. The United States uses about 500 million barrels of oil each year, and in July of 2004, the price of oil reached $40.33 per barrel.

Use the information in the article to answer the following questions.

1. How much would the United States save on oil costs in one year if they used hydroelectricity instead of oil?

   _____

2. About how much would be saved per month?

   _____

3. About how much would be saved per day?

   _____

4. About how much would be saved each minute?

   _____

5. If one Hoover Dam meets the yearly electrical energy needs of 1.3 million people, about how many Hoover Dams would be needed to meet the energy needs of 280,000,000 people in the United States?

   _____

Notes for Home: Your child has learned how to estimate the amount saved when using alternative energy resources.
Home Activity: Help your child estimate savings by calculating the differences in costs between brand-name and generic household products.

Notes

Dear Family,

Your child is learning about the valuable resources on Earth and how we can protect them. In the chapter Protecting Earth's Resources, the class looked at different sources of energy, starting with nonrenewable fuels like coal, crude oil, and natural gas. Then the class studied renewable energy sources, including solar energy, wind energy, and energy from moving water. Other kinds of resources, such as minerals, air, water, and soil were also looked at. Finally, your child learned about ways to protect resources by using less, reusing, and recycling.

Your child has learned many new vocabulary words that describe Earth's resources. Help your child to make these words a part of his or her own vocabulary by using them when you talk together about the resources we need every day.

> resource
> renewable resource
> nonrenewable resource
> fossil fuel
> solar energy
> hydroelectric
> geothermal
> biomass

The following pages include activities that you and your child can do together. By participating in your child's education, you will help to bring the learning home.

© Pearson Education, Inc.

Family Science Activity
Resource Check

Use this chart to collect information about the resources your family uses in one day. The average person in the United States throws away 4.4 pounds of material every day. Does your family throw away more or less than the average?

Resources We Use	Things We Throw Away	Things We Recycle

Talk About It

- What surprised you about how your family uses resources?
- Name three things you could do to use less.
- Name three ways you could reuse resources.
- Name three ways you could recycle more.

Vocabulary Practice

Use vocabulary words to complete. Then write the numbered letters to answer the question below.

1. — ◯ — — — — is
        1
produced by sunlight.

2. — — — ◯ — — — — energy comes
          6
from heat deep within Earth.

3. — — — — ◯ energy comes
        4   3
is material that was
recently alive.

4. — — — — ◯ — is formed
              2
from tiny sea organisms over millions of years.

5. A — — — — — — — — — — ◯
                           5
power plant uses moving water to produce energy.

6. Sunlight, moving water, and wind are examples
of — — ◯ — — — — — energy
      7
resources.

What is the most common mineral on Earth?

◯ ◯ ◯ ◯ ◯ ◯ ◯
1 2 3 4 5 6 7

Can you find the names of ten resources hidden in this puzzle? Use the chart below to classify them.

```
W I N D A G P L E
P E A T R O L S E
P E T R O L E U M
U M U C R D U N E
O I R S O I L C
W L N A L T R E I O
L N G W A T E G P
P W A T E R T H P
O A S T R E N T E
        R E E S R
```

Renewable Resources	Nonrenewable Resources

Fun Fact

Paper makes up 40 percent of what we throw away in the United States. If everyone recycled 10 percent of the newsprint, we would save about 25 million trees every year!

Name _____

The vocabulary words for Chapter 11 are listed in the first column of the chart. Before you read the chapter, write what you think each word means in the second column. After you finish the chapter, write the definition of the word from your textbook in the third column.

Vocabulary Word	What I think the word means	Definition of the word
element		
atom		
proton		
neutron		
electron		
compound		
saturated		
concentrated		
dilute		

Notes for Home: Your child learned the vocabulary words for Chapter 11.
Home Activity: Have your child use the vocabulary words to explain the differences among electrons, neutrons, and protons.

Name _____

⊙ Predict

Science Challenge

You have been assigned the task of placing a set of objects in order from the object with least mass to the object with most mass. The objects are

- a tennis ball
- a toy car
- a regular-sized basketball
- a paper clip
- a new pencil

You do not have a balance to help you find the mass of each object. You will have to predict each mass instead.

© Pearson Education, Inc.

Apply It!

Fill in the graphic organizer. In the box on the left, write what you know about mass. In the box on the right, write your prediction about how the objects should be ordered from the object with least mass to the object with most mass.

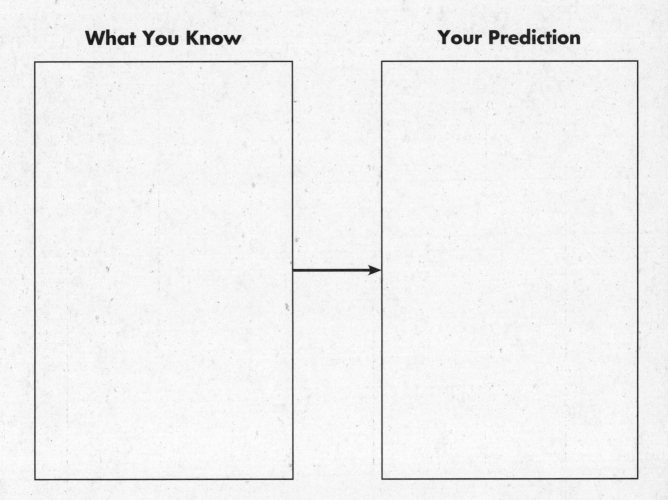

What You Know   **Your Prediction**

© Pearson Education, Inc.

Notes for Home: Your child learned how to make predictions.
Home Activity: With your child, make a small boat out of aluminum foil. Place the boat in a bowl of water. Together predict how many coins it will take to sink the boat.

Notes

Lesson 1: What are properties of matter?

Before You Read Lesson 1

Read each statement below. Place a check mark in the circle to indicate whether you agree or disagree with the statement.

		Agree	Disagree
1.	Elements make up matter.	○	○
2.	The mass of an object changes when it has been moved.	○	○
3.	Density is an example of a chemical property of an object.	○	○
4.	An object will float if its density is less than the liquid's density.	○	○

After You Read Lesson 1

Reread each statement above. If the lesson supports your choice, place a check mark in the *Correct* circle. Then explain how the text supports your choice. If the lesson does not support your choice, place a check mark in the *Incorrect* circle. Then explain why your choice is wrong.

		Correct	Incorrect
1.	_____	○	○
	_____		
2.	_____	○	○
	_____		
3.	_____	○	○
	_____		
4.	_____	○	○
	_____		

Notes for Home: Your child has completed a pre/post inventory of key concepts in the lesson.
Home Activity: With your child, calculate the volumes of several household objects.

Reviewing Terms: Matching

Match each definition with the correct term. Write the letter on the line next to the definition.

_____ 1. properties that describe how a material changes into other materials

_____ 2. properties that can be measured without changing the material

_____ 3. basic kinds of matter

a. chemical properties

b. elements

c. physical properties

Reviewing Concepts: Sentence Completion

Complete each sentence with the correct word or phrase.

_____ 4. Most elements are _____. (metals, pure)

_____ 5. The _____ of an object changes when the pull of gravity changes. (mass, weight)

_____ 6. Use a _____ when measuring the mass of an object. (balance, spring scale)

_____ 7. The density of one liter of olive oil is _____ what it is for four liters of olive oil. (the same as, less than)

_____ 8. If an object's density is _____ a liquid's density, the object will float. (greater than, less than)

Applying Strategies: Calculate

Show all work in completing the answer to question 9. (2 points)

9. What is the formula for calculating the volume of an object? If a gift box is 7 cm long, 4 cm wide, and 3 cm tall, what is its volume?

Lesson 2: How do atoms combine?

Before You Read Lesson 2

Read each statement below. Place a check mark in the circle to indicate whether you agree or disagree with the statement.

		Agree	Disagree
1.	Atoms can be viewed with microscopes.	○	○
2.	Electrons have a negative charge.	○	○
3.	In a periodic table, elements in the same column have similar qualities.	○	○
4.	All compounds are made by sharing electrons.	○	○

After You Read Lesson 2

Reread each statement above. If the lesson supports your choice, place a check mark in the *Correct* circle. Then explain how the text supports your choice. If the lesson does not support your choice, place a check mark in the *Incorrect* circle. Then explain why your choice is wrong.

		Correct	Incorrect
1.	_____	○	○
	_____		
2.	_____	○	○
	_____		
3.	_____	○	○
	_____		
4.	_____	○	○
	_____		

Notes for Home: Your child has completed a pre/post inventory of key concepts in the lesson.
Home Activity: Look at a periodic table of elements. Have your child tell you the names and numbers of protons of some common elements.

Reviewing Terms: Matching

Match each term with the correct definition. Write the letter on the line next to the term.

_____ 1. atom

_____ 2. compound

_____ 3. electron

_____ 4. neutron

_____ 5. proton

a. the part of an atom's nucleus that is positively charged

b. the smallest particle of an element that has the properties of the element

c. a negatively charged particle that moves around the nucleus of an atom

d. the particle in the nucleus with no electrical charge

e. a type of matter made up of a combination of elements

Reviewing Concepts: Sentence Completion

Complete each sentence with the correct word or phrase.

_____ 6. Elements are arranged in a table called the _____ table. (element, periodic)

_____ 7. Atoms in molecules _____ electrons. (share, lose)

_____ 8. All salts can form _____. (molecules, crystals)

Writing

Use complete sentences to answer question 9. (2 points)

9. What does the statement "The properties of salts are different from the properties of the elements that go into making them" mean? Include an example in your answer.

_____

_____

_____

_____

_____

© Pearson Education, Inc.

Lesson 3: How do phase changes occur?

Before You Read Lesson 3

Read each statement below. Place a check mark in the circle to indicate whether you agree or disagree with the statement.

		Agree	Disagree
1.	Unlike liquids, solids have their own volume and shape.	○	○
2.	The freezing point of a liquid is a chemical property.	○	○
3.	In gases, the atoms or molecules are far apart.	○	○
4.	The boiling point of a liquid changes with the amount of liquid.	○	○

After You Read Lesson 3

Reread each statement above. If the lesson supports your choice, place a check mark in the *Correct* circle. Then explain how the text supports your choice. If the lesson does not support your choice, place a check mark in the *Incorrect* circle. Then explain why your choice is wrong.

		Correct	Incorrect
1.	_____	○	○
	_____		
2.	_____	○	○
	_____		
3.	_____	○	○
	_____		
4.	_____	○	○
	_____		

Notes for Home: Your child has completed a pre/post inventory of key concepts in the lesson.
Home Activity: With your child, think about when and where you can see the processes of evaporation and condensation occurring.

Reviewing Concepts: True or False

Write **T** (True) or **F** (False) on the line before each statement.

_____ 1. Three states of matter are solids, liquids, and gases.

_____ 2. Forces between particles in a solid keep them from changing position.

_____ 3. Liquids take the shape of their container.

_____ 4. The freezing point of water can be lowered with the addition of salt.

_____ 5. Gases have a definite shape and volume.

_____ 6. Chilling a liquid will increase evaporation at the surface.

_____ 7. The boiling point of one liter of water is different from the boiling point of two liters of water.

_____ 8. Water vapor and steam are the same thing.

Applying Strategies: Predict

Use complete sentences to answer question 9. (2 points)

9. You take a cold can of juice from the refrigerator on a hot day. Predict whether condensation or evaporation will take place on the outside of the can. Explain.

_____

_____

_____

© Pearson Education, Inc.

Name _____

Lesson 4: What are mixtures and solutions?

Before You Read Lesson 4

Read each statement below. Place a check mark in the circle to indicate whether you agree or disagree with the statement.

	Agree	Disagree
1. Different materials do not form compounds in mixtures.	○	○
2. Metals can be mixtures of different elements.	○	○
3. Water is called the universal solute because it dissolves in many substances.	○	○
4. A solution is concentrated when it is not even close to being saturated.	○	○

After You Read Lesson 4

Reread each statement above. If the lesson supports your choice, place a check mark in the *Correct* circle. Then explain how the text supports your choice. If the lesson does not support your choice, place a check mark in the *Incorrect* circle. Then explain why your choice is wrong.

	Correct	Incorrect
1. _____ _____	○	○
2. _____ _____	○	○
3. _____ _____	○	○
4. _____ _____	○	○

Notes for Home: Your child has completed a pre/post inventory of key concepts in the lesson.
Home Activity: With your child, make solutions by adding ingredients, such as sugar, salt, and flour, to water. Find out which ingredients dissolve and which do not.

Reviewing Terms: Matching

Match each definition with the correct term. Write the letter on the line next to the definition.

_____ 1. little solute in a solution in comparison with the amount of solvent

_____ 2. a solution that contains all the solute that can be dissolved without changing the temperature

_____ 3. a solution with so much solute that it is close to being saturated

a. concentrated

b. dilute

c. saturated

Reviewing Concepts: Sentence Completion

Complete each sentence with the correct word or phrase.

_____ 4. In a _____, materials are placed together but do not form a bond. (compound, mixture)

_____ 5. Materials in a simple mixture can be _____ because they have different properties. (separated, combined)

_____ 6. Bronze and brass are examples of a type of mixture called a(n) _____. (alloy, salt)

_____ 7. When something _____, particles of it separate and spread throughout a solvent. (dissolves, becomes concentrated)

_____ 8. Solubility can be increased by _____. (stirring, adding more solute)

Applying Strategies: Summarize

Use complete sentences to answer question 9. (2 points)

9. What is a solution?

_____

_____

State Temperatures

Different locations in the United States have different climates. The hottest temperature ever recorded in the United States was 134°F in Greenland Ranch, California. The coldest temperature ever recorded was about –80°F in northern Alaska.

Use the tables and line plot to answer the following questions.

State	Extreme Low	Extreme High
Alaska	–80°F	100°F
Arizona	–40°F	128°F
California	–45°F	134°F
Florida	–2°F	109°F
Hawaii	12°F	100°F

State	Extreme Low	Extreme High
Illinois	–36°F	117°F
New York	–52°F	108°F
North Carolina	–34°F	110°F
North Dakota	–60°F	121°F
Texas	–23°F	120°F

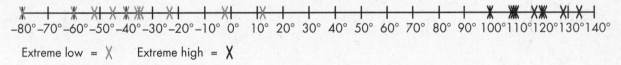

–80° –70° –60° –50° –40° –30° –20° –10° 0° 10° 20° 30° 40° 50° 60° 70° 80° 90° 100° 110° 120° 130° 140°

Extreme low = X   Extreme high = X

1. In which range do the extreme low temperatures cluster?

    _____

2. In which range do the extreme high temperatures cluster?

    _____

3. For what other kinds of data would line plots be a useful tool?

    _____

    _____

Notes for home: Your child learned how to analyze data using tables and line plots.
Home Activity: Help your child find extreme high and extreme low temperatures for locations in South America. Add this data to the line plot and make comparisons.

Notes

Dear Family,

Your child is learning about matter and its properties. The class learned about the physical properties of matter, including color, texture, density, buoyancy. Then they studied how atoms make up all of the elements and compounds. Your child studied the three phases of matter: solid, liquid, and gas. Finally, the class looked at mixtures and solutions.

Your child will learn many new vocabulary words that describe matter. Help your child to make these words a part of his or her own vocabulary by using them when you talk together about elements, compounds, mixtures, and solutions.

> element
> atom
> proton
> neutron
> electron
> compound
> saturated
> concentrated
> dilute

The following pages include activities that you and your child can do together. By participating in your child's education, you will help to bring the learning home.

Family Science Activity

Density of an Orange

Try this experiment to explore the density of an orange. Use the chart to record your observations.

Materials:

- an orange
- a bowl of water
- a knife

Steps

1. Place the orange in a bowl of water. What happens?
2. Carefully peel the orange.
3. Now place the peel in the water. What happens?
4. Finally, place the peeled orange in the water. What happens?

Whole Orange	Orange Peel	Peeled Orange

Talk About It

Which part of an orange is denser than water?
Which part of an orange is less dense than water?
Do you think the results would be the same if you used oil instead of water? Why or why not?

Vocabulary Practice

Matter and Its Properties

Circle the nine vocabulary words in this puzzle. Then write the remaining letters to spell a fact about a special element. Write the letters in order from left to right and top to bottom.

```
D C D I A E M
I O O N S L R
L N N S A E D
U C E C P R U
E E N T L U C
T R R O E T S
A O O T M A R
O R T O E R C
L A N N R M M
D E E D T A O
N T N C N O P
A D R B O N D
```

_____

_____

_____

Answer: Diamonds are solid carbon.

Literacy and Art

Look at the bottles and words.
Draw a picture in each bottle to show solutions.

dilute solution

concentrated solution

saturated solution

Fun Fact

Dry ice is frozen carbon dioxide. At room temperature, it changes from a solid to a gas. This gas looks like smoke. They use dry ice in movies and rock concerts!

Use these vocabulary words to complete the crossword puzzle.

chemical change	polymer	physical change	reactant
chemical equation	product	combustion	

Down

1. substance made during a chemical reaction
2. when a substance changes into another substance with other properties
3. a large molecule made of many smaller units that repeat

Across

4. a scientific "sentence" used to show what happens during a chemical reaction
5. when something is burning, this occurs
6. when a substance changes in size, shape, volume, or phase
7. substance used in a reaction

Notes for Home: Your child learned the vocabulary words for Chapter 12.
Home Activity: Have your child use the vocabulary words to explain the relationships among a chemical reaction, reactants, and products.

Draw Conclusions

Danger to the Ozone Layer

Chlorofluorocarbon (CFC) is a chemical compound containing chlorine, fluorine, and carbon. The first CFC was made in 1892 by a man named Thomas Midgley.

Chlorofluorocarbons are odorless, nontoxic, and nonflammable. They have been used in aerosol cans, refrigerators, and air conditioners. Today we know that they are responsible for some destruction of the ozone layer.

The ozone layer is a layer of ozone gas in Earth's atmosphere. It absorbs most of the harmful ultraviolet radiation that comes from the Sun. Most living things could not survive on Earth without the protection of the ozone layer.

Apply It!

Use the graphic organizer to draw a conclusion that answers this question: What can we do to protect the ozone layer?

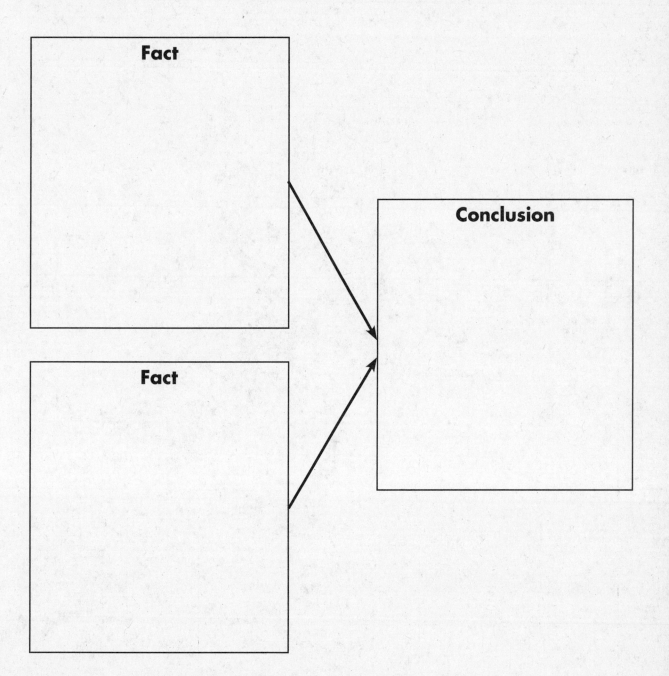

Fact

Fact

Conclusion

Notes for Home: Your child learned how to draw conclusions.
Home Activity: With your child, light a candle and talk about the reaction that is taking place. Have your child draw a conclusion about what would happen if you let the candle continue burning.

Notes

Name _____

Lesson 1: What are chemical changes?

Before You Read Lesson 1

Read each statement below. Place a check mark in the circle to indicate whether you agree or disagree with the statement.

		Agree	Disagree
1.	Physical changes can change the chemical properties of a substance.	○	○
2.	When iron rusts, a chemical change has occurred.	○	○
3.	It is always obvious when a substance undergoes a chemical change.	○	○
4.	The formation of chemical bonds requires a change in energy.	○	○

After You Read Lesson 1

Reread each statement above. If the lesson supports your choice, place a check mark in the *Correct* circle. Then explain how the text supports your choice. If the lesson does not support your choice, place a check mark in the *Incorrect* circle. Then explain why your choice is wrong.

		Correct	Incorrect
1.	_____	○	○
	_____		
2.	_____	○	○
	_____		
3.	_____	○	○
	_____		
4.	_____	○	○
	_____		

Notes for Home: Your child has completed a pre/post inventory of key concepts in the lesson.
Home Activity: Have your child explain to you what happens when iron rusts.

Name _____

Reviewing Terms: Matching

Match each definition with the correct term. Write the letter on the line next to the definition.

_____ 1. one substance changes into a completely different kind of matter

_____ 2. a change occurs but the material keeps its identity

_____ 3. the process of burning

a. chemical change

b. combustion

c. physical change

Reviewing Concepts: True or False

Write **T** (True) or **F** (False) on the line before each statement.

_____ 4. A change in shape or phase of matter is a physical change.

_____ 5. The properties of a substance do not change in a chemical change.

_____ 6. When some kinds of antacid tablets are added to water, the resulting fizz gives off oxygen gas.

_____ 7. Atoms become rearranged in chemical changes.

_____ 8. Formation and breaking of bonds involves taking in or giving off energy.

Applying Strategies: Draw Conclusions

Show all work to answer question 9. (2 points)

9. At 6 P.M., you see logs piled up for a campfire. Later you see flames and feel heat from it. At 8 P.M., only smoldering ashes remain. What changes have taken place? How can you tell?

_____

_____

_____

_____

© Pearson Education, Inc.

Lesson 2: What are some kinds of chemical reactions?

Before You Read Lesson 2

Read each statement below. Place a check mark in the circle to indicate whether you agree or disagree with the statement.

	Agree	Disagree
1. Products are made as a result of a chemical reaction.	○	○
2. Reactants are placed on the right side of a chemical equation.	○	○
3. Matter can be created during a chemical reaction.	○	○

After You Read Lesson 2

Reread each statement above. If the lesson supports your choice, place a check mark in the *Correct* circle. Then explain how the text supports your choice. If the lesson does not support your choice, place a check mark in the *Incorrect* circle. Then explain why your choice is wrong.

	Correct	Incorrect
1. _____ _____	○	○
2. _____ _____	○	○
3. _____ _____	○	○

Notes for Home: Your child has completed a pre/post inventory of key concepts in the lesson.
Home Activity: With your child, think of an analogy or a model to use to explain the different kinds of chemical reactions.

Name _____

Reviewing Terms: Matching

Match each definition with the correct term. Write the letter on the line next to the definition.

_____ 1. a substance used in a chemical reaction

_____ 2. a substance made during a chemical reaction

_____ 3. a formula that describes what happens during a chemical reaction

a. chemical equation

b. product

c. reactant

Reviewing Concepts: Sentence Completion

Complete each sentence with the correct word.

_____ 4. Reactants are always listed on the _____ side of a chemical equation. (right, left)

_____ 5. The Law of Conservation of Mass states that _____ cannot be created or destroyed during a chemical reaction. (matter, reactants)

_____ 6. In a _____ reaction, elements or compounds come together to form new compounds. (decomposition, combination)

_____ 7. Compounds split apart to form smaller compounds in a _____ reaction. (decomposition, combination)

_____ 8. In _____ reactions, one or more compounds split apart and switch places. (replacement, combination)

Applying Strategies: Calculating

Write the correct number on the line before the question. (2 points)

9. _____ How many atoms of hydrogen are in $2H_2O$?

_____ How many atoms of oxygen are in $2H_2O$?

_____ How many atoms of aluminum are in $2Al_2O_3$?

_____ How many atoms of oxygen are there in $2Al_2O_3$?

© Pearson Education, Inc.

Name _____

Lesson 3: How are chemical properties used?

Before You Read Lesson 3

Read each statement below. Place a check mark in the circle to indicate whether you agree or disagree with the statement.

	Agree	Disagree
1. Scientists use the chemical properties of vinegar to dissolve limestone surrounding fossils.	○	○
2. Chemical properties cannot be used to separate a solution.	○	○
3. Indicator paper is used to identify acids and bases.	○	○
4. In a flame test, different substances have the same color flame.	○	○

After You Read Lesson 3

Reread each statement above. If the lesson supports your choice, place a check mark in the *Correct* circle. Then explain how the text supports your choice. If the lesson does not support your choice, place a check mark in the *Incorrect* circle. Then explain why your choice is wrong.

	Correct	Incorrect
1. _____ _____	○	○
2. _____ _____	○	○
3. _____ _____	○	○
4. _____ _____	○	○

Notes for Home: Your child has completed a pre/post inventory of key concepts in the lesson.
Home Activity: Help your child draw a chart and list the ways in which chemical properties can be used to identify materials.

Workbook

Reviewing Concepts: True or False

Write **T** (True) or **F** (False) on the line before each statement.

_____ 1. Chemical properties cannot be used to separate substances.

_____ 2. Limestone can be separated from fossils through the use of vinegar.

_____ 3. When iron ore is heated in a blast furnace, the products are pure iron and carbon dioxide.

_____ 4. Chemical properties can be used to separate elements from solutions.

_____ 5. Strong acids or bases react more easily with materials than do weak acids and bases.

_____ 6. Strong acids will turn universal indicator paper purple.

_____ 7. A soap solution would test as a base with universal indicator paper.

_____ 8. In flame tests, different substances cause a flame to have different colors.

Applying Strategies: Make Inferences

Use complete sentences to answer question 9. (2 points)

9. You test two different unknown substances (A and B) using universal indicator paper. Substance A turns the paper orange. Substance B turns the paper red. Are they acids or bases? Why? Which one is stronger?

_____

_____

_____

Name _____

Lesson 4: How is chemical technology used in our lives?

Before You Read Lesson 4

Read each statement below. Place a check mark in the circle to indicate whether you agree or disagree with the statement.

	Agree	Disagree
1. The invention of antibiotics helped cure bacterial diseases.	O	O
2. Materials such as nylon are found in nature.	O	O
3. A polymer is a molecule made of nonrepeating smaller molecules.	O	O
4. Using household cleaners incorrectly can harm you.	O	O

After You Read Lesson 4

Reread each statement above. If the lesson supports your choice, place a check mark in the *Correct* circle. Then explain how the text supports your choice. If the lesson does not support your choice, place a check mark in the *Incorrect* circle. Then explain why your choice is wrong.

	Correct	Incorrect
1. _____	O	O
_____		
2. _____	O	O
_____		
3. _____	O	O
_____		
4. _____	O	O
_____		

 Notes for Home: Your child has completed a pre/post inventory of key concepts in the lesson.
Home Activity: Review with your child the dangers of using household chemicals incorrectly.

© Pearson Education, Inc.

Reviewing Terms: Sentence Completion

Complete the sentence with the correct term.

_____ 1. A _____ is a large molecule made of many identical smaller units connected together. (vitamin, polymer)

Reviewing Concepts: Sentence Completion

Complete each sentence with the correct word or phrase.

_____ 2. By the mid-1940s, _____ had become an important life-saving medicine. (vitamins, penicillin)

_____ 3. _____ has been used in such items as nets, fabrics, and ropes. (Concrete, Nylon)

_____ 4. A _____ may have thousands or millions of units in a single chain. (polymer, vitamin)

_____ 5. Many _____ are made with chemicals found in petroleum. (fabrics, plastics)

_____ 6. By _____ it and adding sulfur, rubber was made usable year-round. (cooling, heating)

_____ 7. Gasoline, kerosene, and diesel oil are separated from _____ at a refinery. (natural gas, petroleum)

_____ 8. Always read the _____ before using a chemical. (advertisement, directions)

Writing

Use complete sentences to answer question 9. (2 points)

9. Describe ways that chemistry has improved health.

_____

_____

_____

Solving Equations About Mass

Solve each equation. Show your work.

1. $x + 30 = 64$

   _____

2. $335 + n = 500$

   _____

3. $157 - x = 37$

   _____

4. $n + 315 = 600$

   _____

5. Combining oxygen with hydrogen in a fuel cell produces water and energy that can power a car. How many grams of hydrogen must be added to 800 g of oxygen to produce 900 g of water?

   _____

   _____

6. Sodium chloride is the chemical name for common table salt. If 762 g of sodium chloride is decomposed to give 300 g of sodium, how much chlorine will be left?

   _____

   _____

Notes for Home: Your child learned how to solve equations with a single variable.
Home Activity: Using problems 1–4 as models, write several algebra problems with a single variable for your child to solve and explain to you.

Notes

Dear Family,

Your child is learning about how matter changes. In the chapter, Changes in Matter, the class explored both physical and chemical changes. The class focused on ways that chemical changes produce different kinds of matter. Finally, your child also learned how chemical technology affects our lives.

In addition, your child has learned many new vocabulary words. Help your child to make these words a part of his or her own vocabulary by using them when you talk together about changes in matter.

> physical change
> chemical change
> combustion
> reactant
> product
> chemical equation
> polymer

The following pages include activities that you and your child can do together. By participating in your child's education, you will help to bring the learning home.

Family Science Activity
Conservation Conversation

Look for chemical changes that happen every day. The kitchen is one source of many reactions, from lighting a match to making pancakes. Whenever your family notices a chemical change happening, talk about how the Law of Conservation of Matter helps you think about the result.

For example, when a log burns in a fireplace, it looks like the matter is getting smaller because the log shrinks. What is really happening is that the matter is changing into other forms. Oxygen and the wood combust and give off ash, heat, light, and gases such as carbon dioxide. Share any questions with your child's teacher.

Chemical Reaction	Reactants	Products
Example: **burning a log**	**wood and oxygen**	**ash, heat, light, gases**

Talk About It

- How can you prove that the amount of matter is the same before and after you burn a log?
- How can atoms change during a chemical reaction?

Vocabulary Practice Puzzle

Find the vocabulary word from page 1 that completes each sentence below.

1. Rust is an example of a _____ change because one kind of matter changes into a different kind of matter.

2. A chemical _____ shows what happens during a chemical reaction.

3. A _____ is a large molecule made of many identical smaller units connected together.

4. A substance used in a chemical reaction is called a _____.

5. The substance made during a chemical reaction is the _____.

6. Rain freezing to become snow is an example of a _____ change.

7. A log burning in a fireplace is undergoing the chemical process of _____.

Answers: 1. chemical; 2. equation; 3. polymer; 4. reactant; 5. product; 6. physical; 7. combustion

© Pearson Education, Inc.

Chemicals in Daily Life

Many chemicals help us live easier and safer lives. Look at the pictures below and write a sentence about how these things help us in our daily lives.

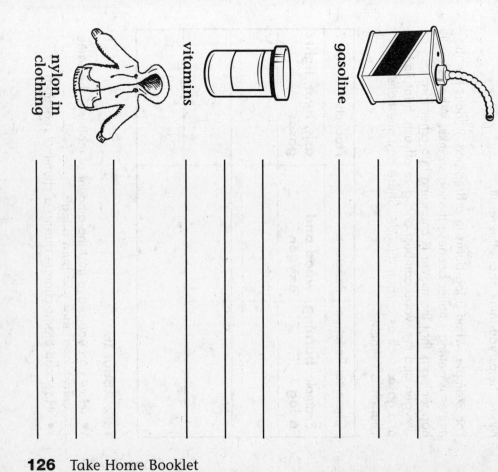

gasoline
_____
_____

vitamins
_____
_____

nylon in clothing
_____
_____

126 Take Home Booklet

Workbook

Find the vocabulary words in the word search puzzle. They may go across, up, down, diagonally, or backward. Then use your textbook to help you match the vocabulary words with their meanings.

| acceleration | work | machine | power |
| equilibrium | force | inertia | velocity |

A	D	E	Q	H	B	F	O	R	C	E	S	G	V
P	N	O	I	T	A	R	E	L	E	C	C	A	E
U	E	E	Q	U	I	L	I	B	R	I	U	M	L
G	N	U	E	S	G	C	Q	O	A	B	J	B	O
D	I	M	I	N	E	R	T	I	A	D	G	M	C
S	H	A	G	X	E	M	P	U	K	R	O	W	I
E	C	I	T	W	S	R	F	C	R	W	T	J	T
N	A	F	O	I	Z	T	A	V	E	L	O	F	Y
I	M	P	C	T	U	J	Y	T	N	E	D	R	S

1. _____: the push or pull on an object

2. _____: the rate at which the velocity of an object changes over time

3. _____: the speed and direction of an object's motion

4. _____: when an object resists any change in motion

5. _____: when forces acting on an object are balanced

6. _____: the energy used when a force moves an object

7. _____: a device that changes the direction or amount of effort needed to do work

8. _____: the speed at which work is done

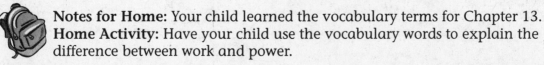

Notes for Home: Your child learned the vocabulary terms for Chapter 13.
Home Activity: Have your child use the vocabulary words to explain the difference between work and power.

⊙ Cause and Effect

Read this science article.

Gravity

You may already know about a force called gravity. This force pulls everything on Earth downward. Without gravity everything would be floating around. You cannot see gravity, but you know it is there because things are not floating around. Gravity is a force that can only pull objects. It is not able to push an object away. This is why objects will always fall to the ground.

A fifth-grade science class tried to see whether gravity would pull a heavy object to the ground faster than a light object. For the light object, they used a piece of paper that they wadded up. They had to crush it tightly into a ball, so that they could reduce the air resistance on the object. For the heavy object, they used a brand-new pencil. One student held the pencil in one hand and the paper ball in the other. The student stretched out her arms in front of her so that they were at the same distance from the ground. Then she dropped both objects at the same time. Both objects hit the ground at the same time. The students concluded that gravity pulls objects at the same rate regardless of weight.

Apply It!

Try the science experiment that is described in the article on page 128. Then fill in the graphic organizer with causes and effects you learned from the article and the experiment.

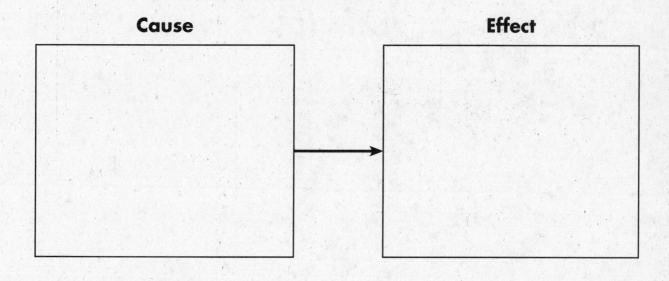

Cause   **Effect**

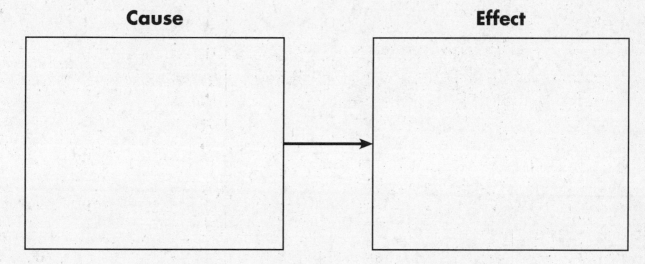

Cause   **Effect**

Notes for Home: Your child learned about determining causes and effects.
Home Activity: With your child, try the experiment in the science article using different pairs of objects you find at home. Chart your results.

Notes

Lesson 1: How can you describe motion?

Before You Read Lesson 1

Read each statement below. Place a check mark in the circle to indicate whether you agree or disagree with the statement.

	Agree	Disagree
1. Parts of your body are always in motion.	○	○
2. Motion is measured by an object's relationship to a frame of reference.	○	○
3. The average speed of an object is measured by dividing time by distance.	○	○
4. If you know the direction an object is moving in, you know its velocity.	○	○

After You Read Lesson 1

Reread each statement above. If the lesson supports your choice, place a check mark in the *Correct* circle. Then explain how the text supports your choice. If the lesson does not support your choice, place a check mark in the *Incorrect* circle. Then explain why your choice is wrong.

	Correct	Incorrect
1. _____ _____	○	○
2. _____ _____	○	○
3. _____ _____	○	○
4. _____ _____	○	○

Notes for Home: Your child has completed a pre/post inventory of key concepts in the lesson.
Home Activity: Have your child calculate the average speed you are moving at during a bike, car, bus, or train ride.

Reviewing Terms: Matching

Match each definition with the correct term. Write the letter on the line next to the definition.

_____ 1. the speed and direction of an object's motion

_____ 2. how far an object moves in a certain amount of time

a. average speed

b. velocity

Reviewing Concepts: True or False

Write **T** (True) or **F** (False) on the line before each statement.

_____ 3. A rubber band has periodic motion when you pluck it.

_____ 4. Different kinds of motion can happen at different rates.

_____ 5. The motion of an object can be measured by looking at it.

_____ 6. Average speed is equal to distance divided by time.

_____ 7. Motion is measured in relationship to a point of reference.

_____ 8. Velocity only describes the direction in which an object is moving.

Applying Strategies: Calculating

9. If you ride your bike 23 kilometers in 1.5 hours, what is your average speed? Show your work. (2 points)

Lesson 2: What are forces?

Before You Read Lesson 2

Read each statement below. Place a check mark in the circle to indicate whether you agree or disagree with the statement.

	Agree	Disagree
1. Forces can make an object move faster or slower or change its direction.	○	○
2. The gravity of all objects, big and small, can be felt.	○	○
3. Unlike electricity and magnetism, gravity can only pull an object.	○	○
4. Work has occurred whether or not an object is moving.	○	○

After You Read Lesson 2

Reread each statement above. If the lesson supports your choice, place a check mark in the *Correct* circle. Then explain how the text supports your choice. If the lesson does not support your choice, place a check mark in the *Incorrect* circle. Then explain why your choice is wrong.

	Correct	Incorrect
1. _____ _____	○	○
2. _____ _____	○	○
3. _____ _____	○	○
4. _____ _____	○	○

Notes for Home: Your child has completed a pre/post inventory of key concepts in the lesson.
Home Activity: With your child, demonstrate examples of static electricity and magnetism in your home.

Reviewing Terms: Matching

Match each definition with the correct term. Write the letter on the line next to the definition.

_____ 1. the energy used when a force moves an object

_____ 2. a push or a pull that acts on an object

_____ 3. the rate at which work is done

a. force

b. power

c. work

Reviewing Concepts: Sentence Completion

Complete each sentence with the correct word or phrase.

_____ 4. The magnitude of a force is measured in _____. (grams, newtons)

_____ 5. An object's _____ is the amount of gravitational force between it and Earth. (mass, weight)

_____ 6. Electrons _____ from one object to another when rubbed together. (move, cannot move)

_____ 7. Friction acts to _____ the motion of an object. (speed up, slow down)

_____ 8. If the force applied to an object doesn't make the object move, then no _____ has been done. (friction, work)

Applying Strategies: Calculating

9. How much work (in Joules) is done when a force of 14 N (Newtons) moves an object 6 meters? (2 points)

Lesson 3: What are Newton's laws of motion?

Before You Read Lesson 3

Read each statement below. Place a check mark in the circle to indicate whether you agree or disagree with the statement.

	Agree	Disagree
1. More than one force can act upon an object at a time.	○	○
2. Balanced forces acting on an object will cause it to change its motion.	○	○
3. Objects with little mass have more inertia than objects with a lot of mass.	○	○
4. Force is equal to an object's mass multiplied by its acceleration.	○	○

After You Read Lesson 3

Reread each statement above. If the lesson supports your choice, place a check mark in the *Correct* circle. Then explain how the text supports your choice. If the lesson does not support your choice, place a check mark in the *Incorrect* circle. Then explain why your choice is wrong.

	Correct	Incorrect
1. _____	○	○
_____		
2. _____	○	○
_____		
3. _____	○	○
_____		
4. _____	○	○
_____		

 Notes for Home: Your child has completed a pre/post inventory of key concepts in the lesson.
Home Activity: Have your child describe Newton's first, second, and third laws in a three-column chart.

Reviewing Terms: Matching

Match each definition with the correct term. Write the letter on the line next to the definition.

_____ 1. a state in which all forces acting on an object are in balance

_____ 2. the tendency of an object to resist any motion

_____ 3. the rate at which the velocity of an object changes over time

a. acceleration

b. equilibrium

c. inertia

Reviewing Concepts: Sentence Completion

Complete each sentence with the correct word.

_____ 4. Change in motion of an object is due to _____ forces acting on it. (balanced, unbalanced)

_____ 5. Newton's _____ law of motion says that an object at rest stays at rest until a net force acts on it. (first, second)

_____ 6. The stronger the force acting on an object, the _____ the object will accelerate. (more, less)

_____ 7. When a person leans against a wall, the wall exerts an _____ and opposite force on the person. (equal, unequal)

_____ 8. Action-reaction forces always occur in _____. (threes, pairs)

Applying Strategies: Cause and Effect

Use complete sentences when answering question 9. (2 points)

9. What is the effect when two teams in a tug-of-war pull with different amounts of force in opposite directions?

_____

_____

Name _____

Lesson 4: What are simple machines?

Before You Read Lesson 4

Read each statement below. Place a check mark in the circle to indicate whether you agree or disagree with the statement.

	Agree	Disagree
1. Machines decrease the amount of work that has to be done.	○	○
2. A pulley makes work easier by changing the direction of the force.	○	○
3. Inclined planes help you use less force over a shorter distance.	○	○
4. A compound machine uses at least two simple machines to do work.	○	○

After You Read Lesson 4

Reread each statement above. If the lesson supports your choice, place a check mark in the *Correct* circle. Then explain how the text supports your choice. If the lesson does not support your choice, place a check mark in the *Incorrect* circle. Then explain why your choice is wrong.

	Correct	Incorrect
1. _____	○	○
_____		
2. _____	○	○
_____		
3. _____	○	○
_____		
4. _____	○	○
_____		

Notes for Home: Your child has completed a pre/post inventory of key concepts in the lesson.
Home Activity: With your child, find simple machines around your home (such as zippers, screwdrivers, and drapery rods). Have your child classify the machines.

Name _____

Reviewing Terms: Sentence Completion

Complete the sentence with the correct term.

_____ 1. A _____ does not reduce the amount of work that has to be done. (force, machine)

Reviewing Concepts: True or False

Write **T** (True) or **F** (False) on the line before each statement.

_____ 2. A simple pulley changes the direction of the force.

_____ 3. A steering wheel in a car is an example of a wheel and axle.

_____ 4. The farther a fulcrum is from the person using a lever, the more difficult the lever is to use.

_____ 5. As the position of the fulcrum changes, the amount of force needed to move a box remains the same.

_____ 6. Without an inclined plane, more force is needed to lift a box straight up.

_____ 7. Wedges and screws are examples of inclined planes.

_____ 8. Complex machines are made up of more than one simple machine.

Writing

Use complete sentences to answer question 9. (2 points)

9. What is a machine? How does a machine affect work that is done?

_____

_____

_____

_____

Gravity, Work, and Power

Force may be measured in newtons (N) where $1 \text{ N} = (1 \text{ kg}) \times (1 \text{ m/s}^2)$. For example, the force needed to accelerate a 1,000-kg automobile at 5 m/s^2 is equal to

$$F = (1,000 \text{ kg}) \times (5 \text{ m/s}^2) = 5,000 \text{ N}$$

Work is measured in joules (J) with 1 joule = (1 newton) × (1 meter). The amount of work done in lifting a 5-N container of water 40 m to the top of a building under construction is

$$W = (5 \text{ N}) \times (40 \text{ m}) = 200 \text{ J}$$

Measured in units of watts, power (P) is the quotient of work divided by time. If the 200 J of work needed to lift the container of water is spread over 20 seconds, then the amount of power expended is

$$P = \frac{(200 \text{ J})}{(20 \text{ S})} = 10 \text{ watts}$$

Use the facts and formulas to answer these problems. Circle your answers.

1. A meteorite weighs 300 N on the Moon. The Moon's "force of gravity" is $\frac{1}{6}$ that of Earth. What is the meteorite's weight on Earth?
    A. 50 N   **C.** 1,800 N
    B. 180 N   **D.** 3,000 N

2. How much work is done by a weightlifter while lifting a 2,000-N barbell 2.5 m?
    A. 800 N   **C.** 5,000 N
    B. 800 J   **D.** 5,000 J

3. How much power does a weightlifter exert in doing 6,000 J of work in 3 seconds?
    A. 2,000 watts   **C.** 6,003 watts
    B. 6,000 watts   **D.** 18,000 watts

Notes for Home: Your child learned about force, work, and energy; the units used to measure them; and how each is calculated.
Home Activity: Help your child find and read short biographies of Joule, Newton, and Watt, the scientists for whom the units are named.

Notes

Dear Family,

Your child is learning about forces in motion. In the science chapter Forces in Motion, we learned how to use speed and velocity to describe motion. Then, we looked at many kinds of forces, including gravity, magnetism, and friction. Finally, after studying Newton's three laws of motion, we looked at simple machines such as the pulley, lever, wheel and axel, and inclined plane.

Your child has learned many new vocabulary words that describe forces. Help your child to make these words a part of his or her own vocabulary by using them when you talk together about the forces you see or use every day.

velocity
force
work
power
equilibrium
inertia
acceleration
machine

The following pages include activities that you and your child can do together. By participating in your child's education, you will help to bring the learning home.

Family Science Activity

Search for Simple Machines

There are simple machines in every room in your house. Use this chart to describe them. Then, try a family scavenger hunt to find other examples of the simple machines around you.

Machine	Is it a pulley, lever, wheel and axel, inclined plane?	How does it work?
refrigerator door	lever	The door moves on a hinge. The hinge is the fulcrum of the lever.
stairs		
doorknob		
clothesline		

Vocabulary Practice

Forces in Motion

Unscramble the letters to find a vocabulary word.
Use the circled letters to answer the riddle.

W K R O

○ — —
10

R P E O W

— ○ — ○ — —
13   3

O C E R F

— — ○ — —
8

I T A R N E

— — — — — —

H I A N C E M

— ○ — — — — —
14

O V Y C I T E L

○ — — — — ○ — —
1   12
9 2

I B E U R Q I M U I L

— — — — ○ — — ○ — — — ○ —
5   7   6   11

T I C R O A N L E C E A

What do you call movement in many directions
and at many speeds?

○ ○ ○ ○ ○ ○ ○ ○
1 2 3 4 5 6 7 8

○ ○ ○ ○ ○ ○
9 10 11 12 13 14

Answer: Variable Motion

Workbook

Use the vocabulary terms to complete the definition sentences. Write one letter in each blank. Use the numbered letters to figure out the secret word.

potential energy	convection	kinetic energy
conduction	energy	radiation

1. The ability to cause a change is called ___ ___ ___ ___ ___ ___.

6

2. Energy due to motion is called

___ ___ ___ ___ ___ ___ ___ ___ ___ ___ ___ ___ ___ ___.

1

3. The transfer of heat by a moving liquid or gas is called

___ ___ ___ ___ ___ ___ ___ ___ ___ ___.

3

4. Energy that is stored is called

___ ___ ___ ___ ___ ___ ___ ___ ___ ___ ___ ___ ___ ___ ___ ___.

5

5. The transfer of heat between two objects touching is called

___ ___ ___ ___ ___ ___ ___ ___ ___ ___.

2

6. The transfer of heat by infrared rays is called

___ ___ ___ ___ ___ ___ ___ ___ ___.

4

Secret Word:

Sound, light, electricity, and magnetism are types of

___ ___ ___ ___ ___ ___.
1   2   3   4   5   6

Notes for Home: Your child learned the vocabulary terms for Chapter 14.
Home Activity: Have your child give examples of kinetic energy and potential energy.

 **Predict**

Read the science story.

A Sound Experiment

A class of fifth graders knew that sound travels in waves, that their ears take in the waves, and that the waves get transferred to the brain. They were not sure if the brain could tell which sound was which. So they performed an experiment to find out if their ears really could detect different sounds.

The class divided into two groups, Group A and Group B. Group A went out of the room. Group B took five plastic eggs and filled each egg with a different material. They filled egg 1 with rice, egg 2 with dried beans, egg 3 with paper clips, egg 4 with popcorn kernels, and egg 5 with pennies. Then each student from Group A came back into the room and partnered with one of the students from Group B. The students in Group B shook each egg near the ears of the Group A students. The Group A students listened very closely to see if they could tell which eggs were filled with which material. The Group A students recorded their guesses on a sheet of paper.

Name _____

Apply It!

Predict the results of the experiment described on page 138. Write what you know in the box on the left and what you think will happen in the box on the right.

What You Know   **Prediction**

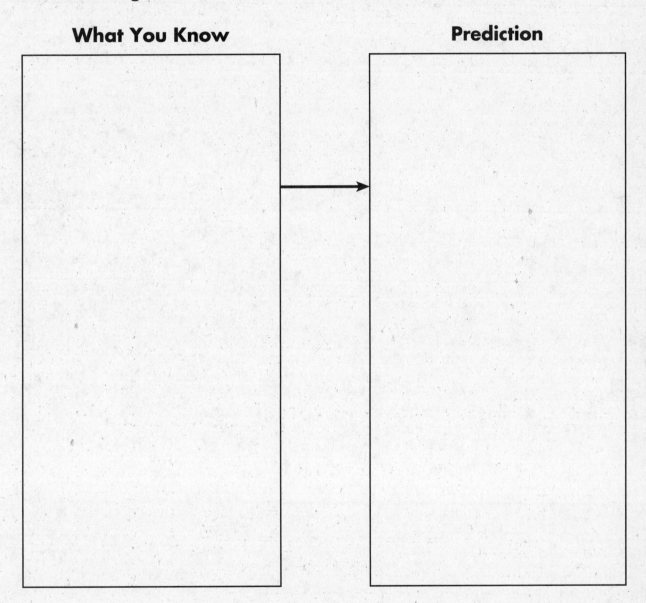

Notes for Home: Your child learned how to predict outcomes based on data.
Home Activity: Cook pasta with your child. Before adding the pasta, ask your child to predict what will happen to the boiling water when the pasta is added.

Notes

Lesson 1: What is energy?

Before You Read Lesson 1

Read each statement below. Place a check mark in the circle to indicate whether you agree or disagree with the statement.

		Agree	Disagree
1.	Energy can be created and it can be destroyed.	○	○
2.	If an object is moving, it has kinetic energy.	○	○
3.	Another name for potential energy is stored energy.	○	○
4.	An atom's nucleus holds a large amount of kinetic energy.	○	○

After You Read Lesson 1

Reread each statement above. If the lesson supports your choice, place a check mark in the *Correct* circle. Then explain how the text supports your choice. If the lesson does not support your choice, place a check mark in the *Incorrect* circle. Then explain why your choice is wrong.

	Correct	Incorrect
1. _____	○	○
_____		
2. _____	○	○
_____		
3. _____	○	○
_____		
4. _____	○	○
_____		

Notes for Home: Your child has completed a pre/post inventory of key concepts in the lesson.
Home Activity: Have your child demonstrate how an object with more mass has more kinetic energy.

Reviewing Terms: Matching

Match each definition with the correct term. Write the letter on the line next to the definition.

_____ 1. energy due to motion

_____ 2. the ability to do work or cause change

_____ 3. energy that is not causing any changes now but can cause changes in the future

a. energy

b. potential energy

c. kinetic energy

Reviewing Concepts: True or False

Write **T** (True) or **F** (False) on the line before each statement.

_____ 4. Every time energy changes form, some of it is given off as unusable heat.

_____ 5. Slow-moving objects have more kinetic energy than fast-moving objects.

_____ 6. Food is an example of chemical energy.

_____ 7. A toy car sitting at the bottom of a ramp has potential energy.

_____ 8. Energy cannot be created or destroyed.

Writing

Use complete sentences to answer question 9. (2 points)

9. Describe a situation where energy is changed several times and heat, light, and/or sound are released.

_____

_____

_____

_____

Lesson 2: What is sound energy?

Before You Read Lesson 2

Read each statement below. Place a check mark in the circle to indicate whether you agree or disagree with the statement.

	Agree	Disagree
1. The vibrations in materials are responsible for making different sounds.	○	○
2. The lower the frequency of the wave, the higher the pitch of the sound.	○	○
3. Decibels are used to measure a sound's intensity.	○	○
4. When the energy of sound waves is transferred, it becomes electrical energy.	○	○

After You Read Lesson 2

Reread each statement above. If the lesson supports your choice, place a check mark in the *Correct* circle. Then explain how the text supports your choice. If the lesson does not support your choice, place a check mark in the *Incorrect* circle. Then explain why your choice is wrong.

	Correct	Incorrect
1. _____	○	○
_____		
2. _____	○	○
_____		
3. _____	○	○
_____		
4. _____	○	○
_____		

 Notes for Home: Your child has completed a pre/post inventory of key concepts in the lesson.
Home Activity: Have your child draw the sound waves of a high-pitched sound and of a low-pitched sound.

Reviewing Concepts: Sentence Completion

Complete each sentence with the correct term.

_____ 1. _____ is/are a measure of loudness. (Frequency, Decibels)

_____ 2. The measure of how fast particles are vibrating is _____. (crest, frequency)

_____ 3. The back-and-forth motion of an object is a _____. (pitch, vibration)

_____ 4. The greater the frequency is, the higher the _____ of the sound. (vibration, pitch)

_____ 5. As _____ increases, the sound carries more energy. (frequency, loudness)

_____ 6. The areas where particles are close together are called _____. (crests, decibels)

_____ 7. Without _____, sound cannot exist. (decibels, vibrating particles)

_____ 8. For sound to be heard, _____ must first cause the object to vibrate. (speed, energy)

Applying Strategies: Calculating

Show all work to answer question 9. (2 points)

9. If sound travels at 331 m/s through dry air at sea level and at 1531 m/s through salt water, about how many times faster is sound traveling through salt water?

Name _____

Lesson 3: What is light energy?

Before You Read Lesson 3

Read each statement below. Place a check mark in the circle to indicate whether you agree or disagree with the statement.

	Agree	Disagree
1. Similar to sound waves, light waves carry electrical and magnetic energy.	○	○
2. Wavelength is measured from the top of one wave to the top of another wave.	○	○
3. We can see most of the light in the spectrum.	○	○
4. When light enters new material, it will bend.	○	○

After You Read Lesson 3

Reread each statement above. If the lesson supports your choice, place a check mark in the *Correct* circle. Then explain how the text supports your choice. If the lesson does not support your choice, place a check mark in the *Incorrect* circle. Then explain why your choice is wrong.

	Correct	Incorrect
1. _____	○	○
_____		
2. _____	○	○
_____		
3. _____	○	○
_____		
4. _____	○	○
_____		

Notes for Home: Your child has completed a pre/post inventory of key concepts in the lesson.
Home Activity: Have your child make a chart of the colors and their corresponding wavelengths.

Reviewing Terms: Matching

Match each definition or example with the correct term. Write the letter on the line next to the definition or example.

_____ 1. waves with many frequencies and wavelengths

_____ 2. the combination of electrical and magnetic energy

_____ 3. the small part of the spectrum that you can see

_____ 4. a transparent object that bends light of different wavelengths by different amounts

a. electromagnetic radiation

b. visible light

c. prism

d. spectrum

Reviewing Concepts: True or False

Write **T** (True) or **F** (False) on the line before each statement.

_____ 5. Light always travels in straight lines.

_____ 6. Light can be bent or refracted when it hits a new material at an angle.

_____ 7. An object in the path of light waves does not cast a shadow.

_____ 8. When light is absorbed, light energy is transformed into stored energy.

Applying Strategies: Compare and Contrast

Use complete sentences to answer question 9. (2 points)

9. In what ways are sound and light alike and different?

_____

_____

_____

_____

_____

© Pearson Education, Inc.

Lesson 4: What is thermal energy?

Before You Read Lesson 4

Read each statement below. Place a check mark in the circle to indicate whether you agree or disagree with the statement.

	Agree	Disagree
1. When matter is warmed, it gains thermal energy.	○	○
2. Thermal energy can cause matter to experience a change of phase.	○	○
3. Thermal energy will always flow from cooler objects to warmer objects.	○	○
4. Conduction is the transfer of heat by a moving liquid.	○	○

After You Read Lesson 4

Reread each statement above. If the lesson supports your choice, place a check mark in the *Correct* circle. Then explain how the text supports your choice. If the lesson does not support your choice, place a check mark in the *Incorrect* circle. Then explain why your choice is wrong.

	Correct	Incorrect
1. _____	○	○
_____		
2. _____	○	○
_____		
3. _____	○	○
_____		
4. _____	○	○
_____		

 Notes for Home: Your child has completed a pre/post inventory of key concepts in the lesson.
Home Activity: Have your child compare and contrast conduction, convection, and radiation.

Reviewing Terms: Matching

Match each definition with the correct term. Write the letter on the line next to the definition.

_____ 1. transfer of heat between objects that are in contact

_____ 2. the total of all the kinetic and potential energy of the atoms of an object

_____ 3. the transfer of heat by electromagnetic waves

_____ 4. the transfer of heat by a moving liquid or gas

a. conduction

b. convection

c. radiation

d. thermal energy

Reviewing Concepts: Sentence Completion

Complete each sentence with the correct word.

_____ 5. _____ is a measure of thermal energy. (Light, Temperature)

_____ 6. When the kinetic energy of atoms increases, thermal energy _____. (increases, decreases)

_____ 7. A liquid becomes a _____ when its particles have absorbed enough energy to escape the surface. (gas, solid)

_____ 8. Melting ice in your hand is an example of _____. (conduction, convection)

Applying Strategies: Predict

Use complete sentences to answer question 9. (2 points)

9. Predict which way thermal energy will flow when you hold a cup with a hot drink in your hands. Explain.

_____

_____

_____

Using Speed to Estimate Distance and Time

The speed of sound in air is about 330 m/s. Sound travels faster in water than it does in the air. The speed of sound in water is about 1,500 m/s.

Sonar is used in water to both detect and estimate the distances to objects. For example, a submarine can use its sonar units to pick up the sounds of another vessel's engine and propellers and then estimate the distance to that vessel.

Use the information to answer these questions. Circle your answers.

1. A car is 1,500 m away from you. The driver blows the horn. How long does it take the sound to reach your ears?

   A. about 1 second   **C.** about 4.5 seconds

   B. about 3 seconds   **D.** about 6 seconds

2. A submarine's sonar unit sends out a signal that bounces off another vessel and returns to the submarine in a round-trip time of 4 seconds. How far is the other vessel from the submarine?

   A. about 1,500 m   **C.** about 4,500 m

   B. about 3,000 m   **D.** about 6,000 m

3. A submarine sends a sonar signal to another submarine that is 8,000 m away. What is the time span between the sending of the signal and its return to the sonar unit?

   A. about 2.7 seconds   **C.** about 10.7 seconds

   B. about 5.3 seconds   **D.** about 21.3 seconds

Notes for Home: Your child learned about estimating time and distance using speed.
Home Activity: With your child, research dolphins' sonar systems. Then together write and solve problems involving dolphins and their sonar.

Notes

Dear Family,

Your child is learning about the changing forms of energy. In the science chapter Changing Forms of Energy, our class looked at energy in its most common forms, including sound, light, electricity, and magnetism. We also studied chemical energy, nuclear energy, and mechanical energy.

In addition, your child has learned many new vocabulary words that describe energy. Help your child to make these words a part of his or her own vocabulary by using them when you talk together about the energy you use every day.

energy
kinetic energy
potential energy
electromagnetic radiation
thermal energy
conduction
convection

The following pages include activities that you and your child can do together. By participating in your child's education, you will help to bring the learning home.

Family Science Activity

Evaluate Energy

Evaluate the changing forms of energy when you bounce a basketball.

Materials:

- basketball (or other bouncing ball)
- meterstick

Steps

1. Hold the basketball half a meter from the ground. Let the ball drop and measure the height it bounces.

2. Repeat the experiment for other heights. Use this chart to record your findings.

Original Height	Bounce Height
.5 m	
1 m	
1.5 m	
2 m	
2.5 m	

Talk About It

Can you find a relationship between the original height and the bounce height?
Why doesn't the ball bounce back to the original height?
Dropping a ball converts gravitational energy into kinetic energy. What other kinds of energy might be produced when the ball bounces? (Hint: Listen up!)

Vocabulary Practice

Changing Forms of Energy

Complete the puzzle with the vocabulary words.

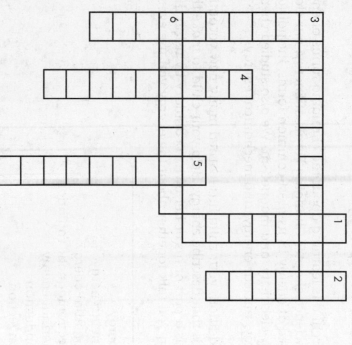

Across

3. Heat moves by _____ when two objects are touching.
6. The total of all the kinetic and potential energy of the atoms in an object is the object's _____ energy.

Down

1. The faster an object moves, the more _____ energy it has.
2. The ability to do work or cause change is _____.
3. The movement of warm liquids or gases to cooler areas is _____.
4. Another name for stored energy is _____ energy.
5. The spectrum of electromagnetic _____ includes visible light as well as other waves, including X-rays, microwaves, and radio waves.

Sound Advice

Experts agree that hearing sounds above 85 db can lead to hearing loss over time. (A handsaw or heavy traffic is about 85 db.) Protect your sense of hearing by reducing your exposure to loud sounds.

Use the vocabulary terms in the box to help you unscramble and write the words. What do you think each vocabulary term means? Write a definition. When you finish reading Chapter 15, check your definitions against those in the text.

circuit diagram	conductor	current	insulator
resistor	volt	electromagnet	

1. udrotccno __ __ __ __ __ __ __ __ __

    Definition: _____

    _____

2. tvlo __ __ __ __

    Definition: _____

    _____

3. tisnluora __ __ __ __ __ __ __ __ __

    Definition: _____

    _____

4. tiiccur gmdiraa __ __ __ __ __ __ __ __ __ __ __ __ __ __

    Definition: _____

5. rrcuetn __ __ __ __ __ __ __

    Definition: _____

    _____

6. gteeternaomlc __ __ __ __ __ __ __ __ __ __ __ __ __

    Definition: _____

7. ssrtorei __ __ __ __ __ __ __ __

    Definition: _____

    _____

Notes for Home: Your child learned the vocabulary terms for Chapter 15.
Home Activity: Have your child use each of the vocabulary terms in an original sentence that explains something about the term.

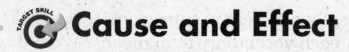

Use with Chapter 15.

Cause and Effect

Read the science article.

Static Electricity

Have you ever walked across the rug,
touched a doorknob, and got a shock?
Maybe you have come inside from the
cold, pulled off your hat, and found
that your hair was standing on end.
These are examples of static electricity.
Once electrons have the same charge,
they repel one another. When you
pull off your hat, you are rubbing the
electrons and making the same charge.
Your hair "stands up" to get away from
other hairs that have the same charge.
Static electricity seems to be more
obvious during the winter. Why? In the
winter the air is very dry. The dry air
allows more electrons to build up, providing you with a shock or
a head of wild hair.

Name _____

Apply It!

An effect can become the cause of another effect, and that effect can in turn become the cause of another effect, and so on, making a chain of causes and effects. Fill in the graphic organizer to show what causes your hair to stand on end. The first and last boxes in the chain are filled in for you.

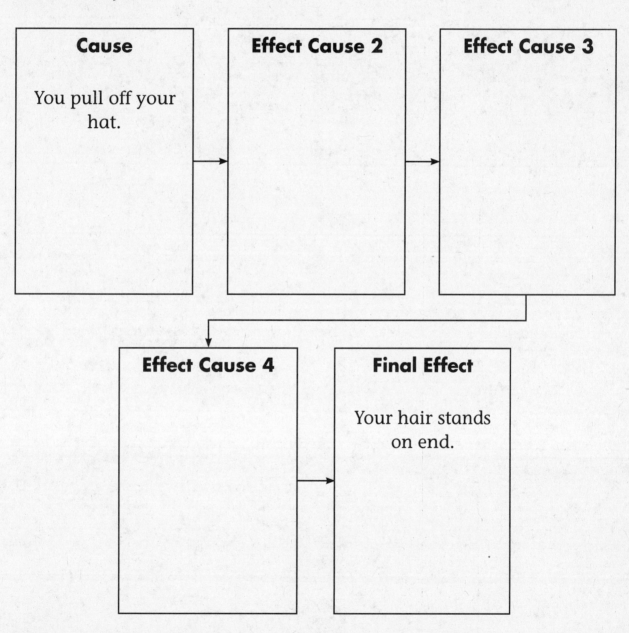

Cause

You pull off your hat.

Effect Cause 2

Effect Cause 3

Effect Cause 4

Final Effect

Your hair stands on end.

Notes for Home: Your child learned about causes and effects.
Home Activity: With your child, charge an empty plastic bottle by rubbing it with a wool sweater or sock. Then turn on a faucet to a steady stream of water, bring the bottle near the water, and watch what happens.

Notes

Lesson 1: What are the effects of moving charges?

Before You Read Lesson 1

Read each statement below. Place a check mark in the circle to indicate whether you agree or disagree with the statement.

		Agree	Disagree
1.	Atoms often lose or gain their protons.	○	○
2.	The flow of charges through a material is the electrical current.	○	○
3.	In conductors, electrons are tightly attached to their atoms.	○	○
4.	Rubber can be used to stop an electrical current.	○	○

After You Read Lesson 1

Reread each statement above. If the lesson supports your choice, place a check mark in the *Correct* circle. Then explain how the text supports your choice. If the lesson does not support your choice, place a check mark in the *Incorrect* circle. Then explain why your choice is wrong.

		Correct	Incorrect
1.	_____	○	○
2.	_____	○	○
3.	_____	○	○
4.	_____	○	○

Notes for Home: Your child has completed a pre/post inventory of key concepts in the lesson.
Home Activity: Have your child explain to you the differences among conductors, resistors, and insulators.

Name _____

Reviewing Terms: Matching

Match each definition with the correct term. Write the letter on the line next to the definition.

_____ 1. a material that resists the flow of an electric charge

_____ 2. the flow of electrical charges through a material

_____ 3. strong resistor through which electric current does not flow

_____ 4. a material through which an electric charge moves easily

a. current

b. conductor

c. resistor

d. insulator

Reviewing Concepts: True or False

Write **T** (True) or **F** (False) on the line before each statement.

_____ 5. Atoms often lose protons but seldom lose or gain electrons.

_____ 6. A surface that loses electrons becomes positively charged.

_____ 7. The flow of charges between two objects is called static electricity.

_____ 8. The plastic or rubber around copper wires is an insulator because it allows the flow of electrons.

Applying Strategies: Cause and Effect

Use complete sentences to answer question 9. (2 points)

9. What characteristic of copper and aluminum causes them to be good conductors? What is the effect of this?

_____

_____

_____

_____

Lesson 2: What are simple circuits?

Before You Read Lesson 2

Read each statement below. Place a check mark in the circle to indicate whether you agree or disagree with the statement.

		Agree	Disagree
1.	Simple circuits have a source of energy, a conductor, a resistor, and a switch.	○	○
2.	Even if a circuit is broken, charges will still flow through it.	○	○
3.	A switch controls the flow of charges.	○	○
4.	Series circuits can only have one resistor on the same wire.	○	○

After You Read Lesson 2

Reread each statement above. If the lesson supports your choice, place a check mark in the *Correct* circle. Then explain how the text supports your choice. If the lesson does not support your choice, place a check mark in the *Incorrect* circle. Then explain why your choice is wrong.

		Correct	Incorrect
1.	_____	○	○
	_____		
2.	_____	○	○
	_____		
3.	_____	○	○
	_____		
4.	_____	○	○
	_____		

Notes for Home: Your child has completed a pre/post inventory of key concepts in the lesson.
Home Activity: Have your child draw and label the parts of a simple circuit.

Reviewing Terms: Matching

Match each definition with the correct term. Write the letter on the line next to the definition.

_____ 1. the source of the energy to move electric charges through a circuit

_____ 2. a map of a circuit

_____ 3. the measure of the electrical energy provided by an energy source

_____ 4. the looped path through which charges move

a. circuit

b. battery

c. circuit diagram

d. volt

Reviewing Concepts: Sentence Completion

Complete each sentence with the correct word.

_____ 5. Current in a circuit is measured in _____. (amperes, volts)

_____ 6. As charge flows in a circuit, some electrical energy always changes to _____ energy. (light, heat)

_____ 7. _____ a switch allows electrical charges to flow in a circuit. (Opening, Closing)

_____ 8. Series circuits always have more than one _____ on a wire. (resistor, conductor)

Applying Strategies: Calculating

9. Using the formula $V/I = R$, find the resistance (ohms) of a CD player where the voltage (V) is 12 volts and the current (I) is 0.2 amps. Show your work. (2 points)

Lesson 3: What are complex circuits?

Before You Read Lesson 3

Read each statement below. Place a check mark in the circle to indicate whether you agree or disagree with the statement.

	Agree	Disagree
1. Parallel circuits have several pathways.	○	○
2. It is safe to unplug cords by yanking on them.	○	○
3. You should stay away from water while using electrical appliances.	○	○
4. The more coils in an electromagnet, the weaker the magnet.	○	○

After You Read Lesson 3

Reread each statement above. If the lesson supports your choice, place a check mark in the *Correct* circle. Then explain how the text supports your choice. If the lesson does not support your choice, place a check mark in the *Incorrect* circle. Then explain why your choice is wrong.

	Correct	Incorrect
1. _____	○	○
2. _____	○	○
3. _____	○	○
4. _____	○	○

Notes for Home: Your child has completed a pre/post inventory of key concepts in the lesson.
Home Activity: With your child, review safety rules for the proper use of the electric appliances in your home.

Reviewing Terms: Matching

Match each definition or example with the correct term. Write the
letter on the line next to the definition or example.

_____ 1. magnets that carry an
electric current

_____ 2. a circuit with several
branches or pathways

    a. parallel circuit

    b. electromagnets

Reviewing Concepts: True or False

Write **T** (True) or **F** (False) on the line before each statement.

_____ 3. Each branch in a parallel circuit may hold several resistors.

_____ 4. All branches in a parallel circuit have to be on at the
same time.

_____ 5. Switches can control each branch in a parallel circuit
separately.

_____ 6. Electrical currents do not always produce a magnetic force.

_____ 7. Electromagnets cannot be made stronger.

_____ 8. Electromagnets can be switched off and on.

Writing

Use complete sentences to answer question 9. (2 points)

9. Steel contains iron. How might an electromagnet be helpful in
sorting steel from other metals at a scrap metal yard?

_____

_____

_____

Name _____

Electrical Measurements: Current, Voltage, and Resistance

If two or more resistors are connected in a series, then the total resistance of the circuit is calculated by adding the Ω values of the individual resistances. This circuit consists of a battery and two resistors connected in a series.

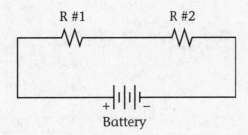

Use the diagram to answer the questions. Circle your answers.

1. If R #1 = 7 Ω and R #2 = 5 Ω, what is the resistance of the circuit?
    A. 5 Ω C. 12 Ω
    B. 7 Ω D. 35 Ω

2. If the total resistance in the circuit is 18 Ω and the current is 0.5 amps, what must the voltage be?
    A. 0.5 V   C. 18 V
    B. 9 V   D. 18.5 V

3. If the voltage is 110 V and the total resistance is 10 Ω, what is the measure of current in the circuit?
    A. 10 amps   C. 100 amps
    B. 11 amps   D. 120 amps

4. What is the current in the circuit if R #1 = 7 Ω, R #2 = 15 Ω, and the voltage is 220 V?
    A. 10 amps   C. 20 amps
    B. 12 amps   D. 242 amps

Notes for Home: Your child learned about circuits and ways of measuring a circuit.
Home Activity: With your child, find and record the voltage, amperes, and/or wattage used by electronic devices in your home. Which have the highest and lowest amperages?

© Pearson Education, Inc.

Notes

Dear Family,

Your child is learning about electricity. In the science chapter Electricity, we have learned how electric charges move through conductors, such as copper, graphite, or salt water. We also learned about materials that resist the flow of electricity. These resistors change some of the electricity to thermal energy. The coils in an electric toaster are good examples of resistors. We also learned about simple and parallel circuits and analyzed diagrams to represent them.

Your child has learned many new vocabulary words to discuss electricity. Help your child to make these words a part of his or her own vocabulary by using them when you talk together about electricity.

> current
> conductor
> insulator
> resistor
> circuit diagram
> volt
> electromagnet

The following pages include activities that you and your child can do together. By participating in your child's education, you will help to bring the learning home.

Family Science Activity
An Electrifying Sketch

Talk about the symbols used to draw a circuit diagram. Look at the box, "Reading a Circuit Diagram," on page 2 of this booklet. Then work together to create a complex circuit diagram. Begin with the battery shown below. Take turns adding parts to the circuit until you have a completed diagram. Trace the flow of electricity with your finger to check your circuit.

Talk About It

How many resistors are there in your circuit?
Is your circuit open or closed?
What happens if a circuit has more than one switch?

Workbook

Which Circuit Is It?

Look at the pictures of the circuits. Which is the simple circuit? The complex circuit? The parallel circuit? Write the type of circuit on the lines.

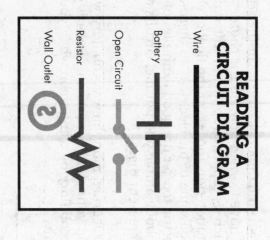

READING A CIRCUIT DIAGRAM

Wire

Battery

Open Circuit

Resistor

Wall Outlet

Fun Fact

On September 4, 1882, the first central power plant opened in New York City. Thomas Edison designed the Pearl Street Station. It had one generator and produced enough electricity for 800 light bulbs.

A circuit with a source of energy and at least one conductor

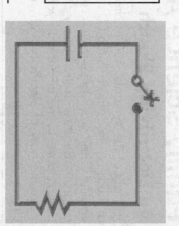

A circuit with more than one resistor on a wire

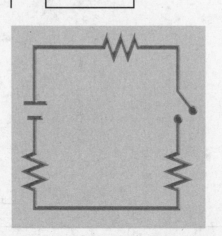

A circuit with more than one branch or pathway

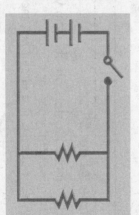

Workbook

Name _____

Use these vocabulary words and clues to fill in the crossword puzzle.

supernova	constellation	black hole
light-year	galaxy	nebula

Across

2. an area in the sky and all of the stars located there

5. a huge system of stars, dust, and gas that is held together by gravity

6. an explosion that is billions of times brighter than a star

Down

1. a point in space with a gravitational field so strong not even light can escape

3. a cloud of gas and dust where a new star is formed

4. the distance that light travels in one year

Notes for Home: Your child learned the vocabulary terms for Chapter 16.
Home Activity: Have your child say, spell, and use the vocabulary terms in original sentences.

© Pearson Education, Inc.

Summarize

Read the science article.

Constellations

Could you imagine how hard it would be to find a specific star in the sky if we did not have constellations? Constellations were first named by farmers and astronomers to help them tell which star was which.

Farmers also used constellations for another reason. By looking at the positions of different constellations, they were able to keep track of the seasons. For example, you can only see the constellation Scorpius in the Northern Hemisphere during the summer. If farmers in the Northern Hemisphere saw Scorpius in the sky, then they would know it was summer. This knowledge helped the farmers figure out which times were the best to plant and harvest their crops.

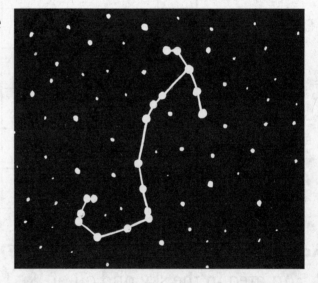

Apply It!

Fill in the graphic organizer to summarize the information in the science article. List three important details. Then write a summary using the details.

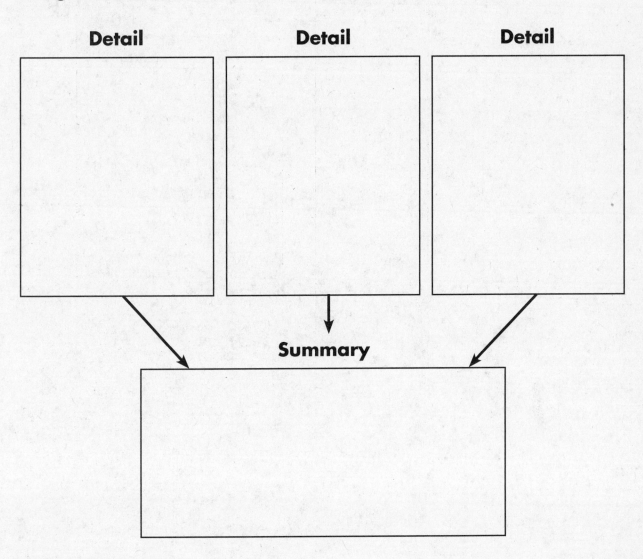

Detail

Detail

Detail

Summary

Notes for Home: Your child learned how to summarize scientific information.
Home Activity: Have your child summarize the plot of a recent movie or television program he or she has seen.

Notes

Name _____

Lesson 1: What is the history of astronomy?

Before You Read Lesson 1

Read each statement below. Place a check mark in the circle to indicate whether you agree or disagree with the statement.

	Agree	Disagree
1. People did not realize that the stars formed patterns until the 1700s.	○	○
2. The astrolabe let people measure the angle between the horizon and a star.	○	○
3. Galileo Galilei invented the telescope.	○	○
4. Telescopes collect and focus the light from objects in the sky.	○	○

After You Read Lesson 1

Reread each statement above. If the lesson supports your choice, place a check mark in the *Correct* circle. Then explain how the text supports your choice. If the lesson does not support your choice, place a check mark in the *Incorrect* circle. Then explain why your choice is wrong.

	Correct	Incorrect
1. _____ _____	○	○
2. _____ _____	○	○
3. _____ _____	○	○
4. _____ _____	○	○

Notes for Home: Your child has completed a pre/post inventory of key concepts in the lesson.
Home Activity: Help your child write a summary of Lesson 1. First decide what the important details are.

© Pearson Education, Inc.

Reviewing Concepts: Sentence Completion

Complete each sentence with the correct word.

_____ 1. Seasons, phases of the Moon, and the rising and setting of the Sun are _____ that are seen in the sky. (stars, patterns)

_____ 2. A _____ eclipse occurs when the Moon blocks the Sun's light. (lunar, solar)

_____ 3. An equinox is the time of year when day and night are of _____ length. (different, equal)

_____ 4. A(n) _____ is a star map drawn on a metal plate. (astrolabe, sextant)

_____ 5. A sextant measures the angle between the _____ and a point in the sky. (horizon, Moon)

_____ 6. Isaac Newton developed a _____ telescope that showed objects in sharper detail. (radio, reflecting)

_____ 7. Telescopes collect and concentrate _____. (light, sound)

_____ 8. Radio telescopes have _____ that collect and focus radio waves. (mirrors, dishes)

Applying Strategies: Summarize

Use complete sentences to answer question 9. (2 points)

9. Summarize Galileo's discoveries in astronomy.

_____

_____

_____

_____

_____

Lesson 2: What is a star?

Before You Read Lesson 2

Read each statement below. Place a check mark in the circle to indicate whether you agree or disagree with the statement.

	Agree	Disagree
1. The Sun is the largest of all stars.	○	○
2. Stars that appear the brightest are also the closest.	○	○
3. Stars that are the hottest are white or blue-white.	○	○
4. Stars go through a long life cycle.	○	○

After You Read Lesson 2

Reread each statement above. If the lesson supports your choice, place a check mark in the *Correct* circle. Then explain how the text supports your choice. If the lesson does not support your choice, place a check mark in the *Incorrect* circle. Then explain why your choice is wrong.

	Correct	Incorrect
1. _____	○	○
_____		
2. _____	○	○
_____		
3. _____	○	○
_____		
4. _____	○	○
_____		

Notes for Home: Your child has completed a pre/post inventory of key concepts in the lesson.
Home Activity: Ask your child to explain the stages during the life cycle of stars.

Name _____

Reviewing Terms: Matching

Match each definition with the correct term. Write the letter on the line next to the definition.

_____ 1. a gigantic explosion of a star millions or billions of times brighter than the star was

_____ 2. a cloud of gas and dust in which new stars form

_____ 3. a point in space with a force of gravity so strong that nothing within a certain distance can escape being sucked in

_____ 4. the distance light travels in one year

a. light year

b. nebula

c. supernova

d. black hole

Reviewing Concepts: True or False

Write **T** (True) or **F** (False) on the line before each statement.

_____ 5. The Sun is the closest star to Earth.

_____ 6. The hottest stars are red stars.

_____ 7. The three layers of the Sun are the photosphere, the chromosphere, and the corona.

_____ 8. A white dwarf star is one that has no fuel to make its own energy.

Applying Strategies: Calculating

9. One light-year is about 9 trillion kilometers. Arcturus is a star that is 37 light-years from Earth. If you are about 11 years old now, how old will you be when light that is leaving Arcturus today reaches Earth? How far, in kilometers, will it have traveled? Show your work. (2 points)

Lesson 3: How are stars grouped together?

Before You Read Lesson 3

Read each statement below. Place a check mark in the circle to indicate whether you agree or disagree with the statement.

	Agree	Disagree
1. Billions of galaxies exist in the universe.	○	○
2. The Milky Way is a spiral galaxy.	○	○
3. No matter where you live in the world, you will see the same constellations.	○	○
4. Constellations actually move across the sky.	○	○

After You Read Lesson 3

Reread each statement above. If the lesson supports your choice, place a check mark in the *Correct* circle. Then explain how the text supports your choice. If the lesson does not support your choice, place a check mark in the *Incorrect* circle. Then explain why your choice is wrong.

	Correct	Incorrect
1. _____	○	○
_____		
2. _____	○	○
_____		
3. _____	○	○
_____		
4. _____	○	○
_____		

Notes for Home: Your child has completed a pre/post inventory of key concepts in the lesson.
Home Activity: With your child, research several common constellations. Have your child draw a map to show the locations of constellations at a specific time of year.

Reviewing Terms: Matching

Match each definition or example with the correct term. Write the letter on the line next to the definition or example. You will use each term more than once.

_____ 1. a huge system of stars, dust, and gas held together by gravity

_____ 2. Scorpius or Ursa Major

_____ 3. an area of the sky and all the stars visible in that area

_____ 4. The Milky Way

   a. constellation

   b. galaxy

Reviewing Concepts: Sentence Completion

Complete each sentence with the correct word or phrase.

_____ 5. A(n) _____ galaxy has a bright, bulging middle and wispy arms fanning out from the center. (elliptical, spiral)

_____ 6. The half of Earth north of the equator is called the _____ Hemisphere. (Northern, Southern)

_____ 7. The Sun seems to travel across the sky because _____ is spinning. (the Sun, Earth)

_____ 8. _____ change with the seasons because Earth is traveling around the Sun. (Constellations, Galaxies)

Writing

Use complete sentences to answer question 9. (2 points)

9. You are stranded on an island and wonder where you are. After a quick look at the sky, you determine that you are in the Southern Hemisphere. How did you conclude this?

_____

_____

_____

Shrinking the Solar System Down to Size

The chart below shows the approximate diameter (rounded to the nearest 100 km) of each planet along with the comparative diameter using a 1,000 km = 1 cm scale.

Planet	Approximate Diameter	Comparative Diameter
Mercury	4,879 km	4.9 cm
Venus	12,104 km	12.1 cm
Earth	12,756 km	12.8 cm
Mars	6,794 km	6.8 cm
Jupiter	142,984 km	142.9 cm
Saturn	120,536 km	120.5 cm
Uranus	51,118 km	51.1 cm
Neptune	49,528 km	49.5 cm
Pluto	2,302 km	2.3 cm

Use the chart to answer the questions. Circle or write your answer.

1. Which planet's diameter is closest to Earth's diameter?
   A. Mercury B. Venus C. Mars D. Pluto

2. Which planet has a diameter that is about four times the diameter of Earth?
   A. Mercury B. Uranus C. Neptune D. Pluto

3. Which planet's diameter is about one-tenth that of Neptune?
   A. Mercury B. Venus C. Mars D. Pluto

Notes for Home: Your child learned how to make large measurements easier to understand.
Home Activity: To help your child understand the relative sizes of the planets, use the diameter measurements (those in centimeters) to cut out corresponding paper lengths.

Notes

Take Home Booklet

Use with Chapter 16

Dear Family,

Your child is learning about stars and galaxies. First we looked at the history of astronomy, from the earliest beliefs about eclipses to later developments by early scientists using unique tools. Then we found out what modern technology has revealed about stars and galaxies. We studied the brightness, color, and temperature of stars as well as their life cycle.

Your child has learned many new vocabulary words that describe parts of the universe. Help your child to make these words a part of his or her own vocabulary by using them when you talk together about the night sky.

> light-year
> nebula
> supernova
> black hole
> galaxy
> constellation

These following pages include activities that you and your child can do together. By participating in your child's education, you will help to bring the learning home.

Family Science Activity

Our Expanding Universe

You and your child can create a model of our expanding universe.

Materials

- balloon (white or light-colored is best)
- 3 markers in different colors
- ruler

Steps

1. Blow up the balloon until it is about the size of a softball. Twist the end and hold it tightly.
2. Invite your child to draw a dot representing Earth. Mark the color in the chart below to help you remember which dot represents Earth.
3. Draw a dot in a different color to represent the nearest star. Put the dot one inch away.
4. Using a third color, add dots around the rest of the balloon to represent other stars.

Color of Earth	Nearest Star	Other Stars

5. Model the expansion of the universe by inflating the balloon until it is about the size of your head.

Talk About It

What happened to the stars as the universe expanded? How could you model a contracting universe using the same tools?

Workbook

Stars and Galaxies

Complete each sentence with a vocabulary word. You may look at the number of letters in each word to help you.

Vocabulary words:

light-years   **black hole**
galaxy   **constellation**

1. A _____ is an area of the sky and all the stars seen in that area.

2. The Milky Way is an example of a _____, a huge system of stars, dust, and gas held together by gravity.

3. A _____ is a point in space that has such a strong force of gravity that nothing within a certain distance of it can escape getting sucked into that point.

4. Because the distances between stars are so huge, scientists measure these distances in _____.

Constellations

Draw in lines to connect the dots for each constellation.
Write the name of each constellation.

Constellations in the picture:
Ursa Major (bear)
Centaurus (a centaur is half-human, half-horse)
Scorpius (scorpion)

Constellations

_____

The vocabulary words in the chapter are in the first column of the chart. Fill in the second column. After you read the chapter, fill in the last column using your book.

Vocabulary Word	What do you think it means?	Definition from the book
solar system		
revolution		
axis		
rotation		
space probe		
comet		
asteroid		
satellite		
Moon phase		

Notes for Home: Your child learned the vocabulary terms for Chapter 17.
Home Activity: Help your child make up a crossword puzzle using the vocabulary terms and the definitions he or she wrote based on the textbook.

⊙ Make Inferences

Read the science article.

Health Risks for Astronauts

Most people know that being an astronaut can be dangerous. But few of them know about the long-term health risks that an astronaut faces. One health problem is bone loss, which can happen to an astronaut who spends months or years in a weightless environment. Another problem is the mental stress of spending time in space. Stress can weaken the immune system's ability to protect the body against disease.

Apply It!

What can you infer about health problems an astronaut might have after spending a long time in space? Fill in the graphic organizer on the next page.

Facts   **Inference**

```
┌─────────────────────┐
│                     │
│                     │  ──────┐
│                     │        │
└─────────────────────┘        │    ┌──────────────────────┐
                               ├──→ │                      │
┌─────────────────────┐        │    │                      │
│                     │        │    │                      │
│                     │  ──────┘    │                      │
│                     │             │                      │
└─────────────────────┘             └──────────────────────┘
```

Notes for Home: Your child learned about making inferences.
Home Activity: Look at the Moon with your child. From your observations, infer how life might be different if you lived on the Moon.

Notes

Lesson 1: In what ways does Earth move?

Before You Read Lesson 1

Read each statement below. Place a check mark in the circle to indicate whether you agree or disagree with the statement.

	Agree	Disagree
1. Planets travel in orbits around the Sun.	○	○
2. One orbit is called a rotation.	○	○
3. When one part of Earth faces toward the Sun, it is daytime.	○	○
4. Distance from the Sun causes Earth's seasons.	○	○

After You Read Lesson 1

Reread each statement above. If the lesson supports your choice, place a check mark in the *Correct* circle. Then explain how the text supports your choice. If the lesson does not support your choice, place a check mark in the *Incorrect* circle. Then explain why your choice is wrong.

	Correct	Incorrect
1. _____	○	○
_____		
2. _____	○	○
_____		
3. _____	○	○
_____		
4. _____	○	○
_____		

Notes for Home: Your child has completed a pre/post inventory of key concepts in the lesson.
Home Activity: Ask your child to explain to you what causes the seasons to change and why there are days and nights.

© Pearson Education, Inc.

Reviewing Terms: Matching

Match each definition with the correct term. Write the letter on the line next to the definition.

_____ 1. the Sun, its nine planets, moons, asteroids, and comets

_____ 2. one full orbit around the Sun

_____ 3. an imaginary center line

_____ 4. one whole spin of an object on its axis

a. axis

b. revolution

c. rotation

d. solar system

Reviewing Concepts: True or False

Write **T** (True) or **F** (False) on the line before each statement.

_____ 5. Earth's elliptical orbit lasts 365 days.

_____ 6. The Moon has an atmosphere just like Earth's atmosphere.

_____ 7. Earth's tilt causes Earth to have seasons.

_____ 8. Light from the Sun transfers energy to Earth.

Writing

Use complete sentences to answer question 9. (2 points)

9. What are some of the ways Earth is protected by its atmosphere?

_____

_____

_____

_____

_____

_____

Name _____

Lesson 2: What are the parts of the solar system?

Before You Read Lesson 2

Read each statement below. Place a check mark in the circle to indicate whether you agree or disagree with the statement.

	Agree	Disagree
1. Gravity is a force that keeps all the planets in their orbits.	○	○
2. Planets closest to the Sun travel the slowest in their orbits.	○	○
3. Earth is the largest planet in our solar system.	○	○
4. Space probes do not have astronauts aboard them.	○	○

After You Read Lesson 2

Reread each statement above. If the lesson supports your choice, place a check mark in the *Correct* circle. Then explain how the text supports your choice. If the lesson does not support your choice, place a check mark in the *Incorrect* circle. Then explain why your choice is wrong.

	Correct	Incorrect
1. _____ _____	○	○
2. _____ _____	○	○
3. _____ _____	○	○
4. _____ _____	○	○

Notes for Home: Your child has completed a pre/post inventory of key concepts in the lesson.
Home Activity: Help your child make a model of the solar system by painting foam balls and suspending them from two crisscrossed hangers.

Reviewing Concepts: Matching

Match each description with the correct planet listed below. Write the correct planet on the line before the description. One planet is not used.

Mercury   Venus   Earth   Mars   Jupiter
Saturn   Uranus   Neptune   Pluto

_____ 1. a gas giant; the largest planet

_____ 2. a deep blue gas planet that gives off more energy than it receives from the Sun

_____ 3. a rocky planet covered by red, dusty soil

_____ 4. a planet with a thick layer of hot clouds covering a rocky surface

_____ 5. the smallest and coldest planet

_____ 6. the least dense of all the planets

_____ 7. the planet that is one Astronomical Unit from the Sun

_____ 8. the blue-green gas giant with an axis tipped farther than any other planet

Applying Strategies: Summarize

Use complete sentences to answer question 9. (2 points)

9. Tell what a space probe is and what it does. Name two space probes and tell to what planet they have been sent.

_____

_____

_____

_____

© Pearson Education, Inc.

Lesson 3: What are comets and asteroids?

Before You Read Lesson 3

Read each statement below. Place a check mark in the circle to indicate whether you agree or disagree with the statement.

		Agree	Disagree
1.	Comets are the same size as planets.	○	○
2.	Asteroids can be hundreds of kilometers wide or as small as a pebble.	○	○
3.	Shooting stars are actually meteors.	○	○
4.	Most asteroids hit Earth.	○	○

After You Read Lesson 3

Reread each statement above. If the lesson supports your choice, place a check mark in the *Correct* circle. Then explain how the text supports your choice. If the lesson does not support your choice, place a check mark in the *Incorrect* circle. Then explain why your choice is wrong.

		Correct	Incorrect
1.	_____	○	○
	_____		
2.	_____	○	○
	_____		
3.	_____	○	○
	_____		
4.	_____	○	○
	_____		

© Pearson Education, Inc.

Notes for Home: Your child has completed a pre/post inventory of key concepts in the lesson.
Home Activity: With your child, review the similarities and differences among comets, asteroids, and meteors. Make a three-column chart to record the information.

Name _____

Reviewing Terms: Matching

Match each definition with the correct term. Write the letter on the line next to the definition.

_____ 1. a rocky mass up to several hundred kilometers wide that revolves around the Sun

_____ 2. a frozen mass of different types of ice and dust that orbits the Sun

a. asteroid

b. comet

Reviewing Concepts: Sentence Completion

Complete each sentence with the correct word or phrase.

_____ 3. _____ comets a year may travel into the solar system and circle the Sun. (Five, Several)

_____ 4. Most comets are found just before _____. (sunset, sunrise)

_____ 5. The _____ and tail of a comet form when it gets close enough to the Sun to melt the nucleus. (coma, nucleus)

_____ 6. Most asteroids orbit the Sun in a region between Mars and Jupiter called the _____ belt. (asteroid, meteorite)

_____ 7. _____ gravity holds most asteroids in the area beyond Mars. (The Sun's, Jupiter's)

_____ 8. Most _____ burn up before they hit Earth's surface. (meteors, asteroids)

Applying Strategies: Calculating

Show all work when answering question 9. (2 points)

9. Asteroid Ida is 58 kilometers long. Asteroid Gaspra is 19 kilometers long. About how many times longer is Ida than Gaspra?

© Pearson Education, Inc.

Name _____

Lesson 4: What is known about the Moon?

Before You Read Lesson 4

Read each statement below. Place a check mark in the circle to indicate whether you agree or disagree with the statement.

		Agree	Disagree
1.	The Moon is a quarter of Earth's size.	○	○
2.	The Moon's surface is smooth and flat.	○	○
3.	The phases of the Moon are caused by the positions of the Moon and Earth.	○	○
4.	The Sun is the main cause of rising and falling tides.	○	○

After You Read Lesson 4

Reread each statement above. If the lesson supports your choice, place a check mark in the *Correct* circle. Then explain how the text supports your choice. If the lesson does not support your choice, place a check mark in the *Incorrect* circle. Then explain why your choice is wrong.

		Correct	Incorrect
1.	_____	○	○
	_____		
2.	_____	○	○
	_____		
3.	_____	○	○
	_____		
4.	_____	○	○
	_____		

 Notes for Home: Your child has completed a pre/post inventory of key concepts in the lesson.
Home Activity: With your child, look at the Moon on a clear night. Have your child identify the Moon's phase and explain why it looks that way.

Reviewing Terms: Matching

Match each definition with the correct term. Write the letter on the line next to the definition.

_____ 1. a moon, rock, or any object that orbits another object

_____ 2. the shapes of the lit side of the Moon that can be seen

_____ 3. the daily rise and fall of the oceans on Earth

a. Moon phases

b. satellite

c. tide

Reviewing Concepts: True or False

Write **T** (True) or **F** (False) on the line before each statement.

_____ 4. The "near side" of the Moon always faces Earth.

_____ 5. The Moon has an atmosphere of air and water like Earth's.

_____ 6. Some craters on the Moon have been caused by crashed space vehicles.

_____ 7. The Moon makes its own light.

_____ 8. Gravity causes Earth's land, water, and atmosphere to bulge slightly toward the Moon.

Applying Strategies: Make Inferences

Use complete sentences to answer question 9. (2 points)

9. In the newspaper one day, you read that the highest tides of the season are expected in the next month. What can you infer about the positions of the Sun, Earth, and the Moon? What phase of the Moon will probably be visible?

_____

_____

_____

_____

© Pearson Education, Inc.

Name _____

Ratios and Gravity

Gravity is measured in units of acceleration. For example, Earth's gravity is about 9.8 meters per second squared (about 32.1 feet per second squared). The second column in the chart below shows the actual gravity on each planet in our solar system. The third column gives the ratio of each planet's gravity to the gravity of Earth. Because this scale is calculated by dividing m/s^2 by m/s^2, the figures in the third column have no units.

Planet	Gravity	Scale Gravity
Mercury	3.70 m/s^2	0.38
Venus	8.87 m/s^2	0.91
Earth	9.78 m/s^2	1.00
Mars	3.70 m/s^2	0.38
Jupiter	20.87 m/s^2	2.13
Saturn	7.21 m/s^2	0.74
Uranus	8.43 m/s^2	0.86
Neptune	10.71 m/s^2	1.10
Pluto	0.81 m/s^2	0.08

Use the chart to answer the questions.

1. Two measurements that are equal are said to have a 1-to-1 ratio (written as 1:1). Which two planets have a 1:1 ratio of gravities?

_____

2. If a rock weighs 100 pounds on Jupiter, what will it weigh on Earth?

_____

Notes for Home: Your child has learned about using ratios to compare gravities on planets.
Home Activity: Help your child find the Moon's gravity and compare it to Earth's gravity. Have your child calculate what his or her weight would be on the Moon.

Notes

Dear Family,

In the chapter Earth in Space, your child is learning about Earth and space. We are studying how Earth's rotation and tilt on its axis create regular patterns, such as day and night, the seasons, and climates. We have studied the other planets in our solar system. We also learned about comets and asteroids, including meteors, meteoroids, and meteorites. Finally, we looked at surface, orbit, and phases.

Your child has learned many new vocabulary words that describe our solar system. Help your child to make these words a part of his or her own vocabulary by using them when you talk together about space.

> axis
> Moon phase
> satellite
> solar system
> space probe
> asteroid
> rotation
> revolution
> comet

The following pages include activities that you and your child can do together. By participating in your child's education, you will help to bring the learning home.

Family Science Activity

Planets on a String

Create a model to show the order of planets.

Materials

- poster board
- marker
- string
- tape
- yardstick
- scissors
- paper clips

Steps

1. Cut nine circles to represent the nine planets.
2. Write the names of the planets.
3. Cut a length of string nine feet long. Use the chart below to mark the positions for each planet. The beginning of the string represents the Sun.
4. Use paper clips to hang each planet in place. Tape the paper clips to the string to keep them from shifting.
5. Have two people hold the ends of the string and walk apart until the string is tight.

Mercury: 1 inch
Earth: 3 inches
Jupiter: 14 inches
Uranus: 4 feet 3 inches
Pluto: 8 feet 10 inches

Venus: 2 inches
Mars: 4 inches
Saturn: 2 feet 2 inches
Neptune: 6 feet 9 inches

Workbook

Vocabulary Practice

Earth in Space

Circle nine vocabulary words in this puzzle. Then write the letters you did not circle in order from upper left to lower right to answer the question.

H	U	B	R	B	S	L	E
A	S	T	E	R	O	I	D
S	P	S	V	O	L	M	P
A	A	A	O	T	A	O	C
A	C	T	L	A	R	O	E
X	E	E	U	T	S	N	T
I	P	L	T	I	Y	P	E
S	R	L	I	O	S	H	L
E	O	I	O	N	T	A	S
C	B	T	N	O	E	S	P
E	E	E	C	O	M	E	T

What important astronomical tool was launched on April 24, 1990?

_____ _____ _____ _____ _____

_____ _____ _____ _____

Solar System Riddles

Solve each riddle.

1. I am a star!
   I am the largest body in the solar system.

   Who am I? _____

2. I have a thousand rings.
   My rings are made of rock, dust, and ice.

   Who am I? _____

Write your own riddle about the solar system.

_____

_____

_____

Fun Fact

People say that something happens "once in a blue moon" to describe something quite unusual. A blue moon is the second full moon in a calendar month. So how unusual is a blue moon? Blue moons will occur in June 2007 and December 2009.

Look through the chapter to find a definition for each vocabulary
word. Then think of an example that helps explain the word.

Vocabulary Word	Definition	Example
technology		
inventor		
manufacturing		
assembly line		
microchip		
World Wide Web		
space station		

© Pearson Education, Inc.

Notes for Home: Your child learned the vocabulary terms for Chapter 18.
Home Activity: Have your child use the vocabulary words to identify and explain
examples of technology at home and in school.

Name _____

Sequence

Read the science article.

The Television Set

One major example of changing technology is the television set. Invented in 1927, the first television set did not have color pictures and was not turned on with a remote control. You could only watch black-and-white images on the screen. Also, there were not many channels for people to watch on the early televisions. The remote control wasn't introduced until 1956. Another big moment in the

history of television occurred in 1966. CBS decided that it would be the first network to broadcast programs in color all the time.

Think about our television sets now. They can be tiny or huge. Flat-screen televisions came out in 1999. These televisions take up much less space than standard models. People can also choose between cable and satellite to provide them with many more television channels. Technology has made a lot of changes to the television set.

Apply It!

Fill in the graphic organizer. In the correct sequence, list the important moments in television technology that you read about on page 178.

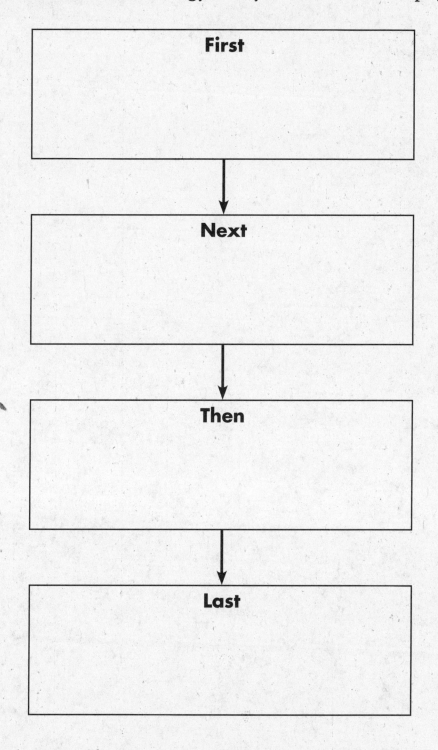

First

Next

Then

Last

Notes for Home: Your child learned how to put events in sequence.
Home Activity: Discuss with your child some of the toys that you played with when you were young. Do any of these toys still exist today?

© Pearson Education, Inc.

Notes

Lesson 1: What is technology?

Before You Read Lesson 1

Read each statement below. Place a check mark in the circle to indicate whether you agree or disagree with the statement.

	Agree	Disagree
1. People use technology to invent new devices or processes.	○	○
2. Technology has only positive effects.	○	○
3. Examples of technology in our homes include microwave ovens and scissors.	○	○
4. The assembly line made manufacturing slower and more expensive.	○	○

After You Read Lesson 1

Reread each statement above. If the lesson supports your choice, place a check mark in the *Correct* circle. Then explain how the text supports your choice. If the lesson does not support your choice, place a check mark in the *Incorrect* circle. Then explain why your choice is wrong.

	Correct	Incorrect
1. _____	○	○
_____		
2. _____	○	○
_____		
3. _____	○	○
_____		
4. _____	○	○
_____		

Notes for Home: Your child has completed a pre/post inventory of key concepts in the lesson.
Home Activity: Discuss with your child what you believe is the most important technological advance and why.

Name _____

Reviewing Terms: Matching

Match each definition with the correct term. Write the letter on the line next to the definition.

_____ 1. the use of scientific knowledge for a purpose

_____ 2. someone who uses technology to develop a new device or process or to solve a problem

_____ 3. a way of building a product in which it moves through a factory as workers add parts to it

_____ 4. the production of goods on a large scale

a. assembly line

b. inventor

c. manufacturing

d. technology

Reviewing Concepts: True or False

Write **T** (True) or **F** (False) on the line before each statement.

_____ 1. Technology can have negative effects.

_____ 2. A cellular phone is an example of technology, but a plastic container is not.

_____ 3. Technology can change society.

_____ 4. An assembly line is a quick but expensive way to build products.

Applying Strategies: Sequence

Use complete sentences to answer question 9. (2 points)

9. Write an assembly line sequence for making 100 peanut butter and jelly sandwiches and getting them wrapped and into boxes.

_____

_____

_____

_____

© Pearson Education, Inc.

Name _____

Lesson 2: How has technology changed transportation?

Before You Read Lesson 2

Read each statement below. Place a check mark in the circle to indicate whether you agree or disagree with the statement.

		Agree	Disagree
1.	Long ago, steam was used to power ships and trains.	○	○
2.	Magnetic force can be used to move trains.	○	○
3.	Years ago, cars were much safer than they are now.	○	○
4.	Pollution from cars is not a problem in our country anymore.	○	○

After You Read Lesson 2

Reread each statement above. If the lesson supports your choice, place a check mark in the *Correct* circle. Then explain how the text supports your choice. If the lesson does not support your choice, place a check mark in the *Incorrect* circle. Then explain why your choice is wrong.

		Correct	Incorrect
1.	_____	○	○
	_____		
2.	_____	○	○
	_____		
3.	_____	○	○
	_____		
4.	_____	○	○
	_____		

Notes for Home: Your child has completed a pre/post inventory of key concepts in the lesson.
Home Activity: With your child, compare and contrast the negative and positive effects of the invention of the automobile.

© Pearson Education, Inc.

Workbook

Reviewing Concepts: Sentence Completion

Complete each sentence with the correct word or phrase.

_____ 1. _____ engines first operated many kinds of machines in factories. (Gasoline, Steam)

_____ 2. Modern ships use _____ engines to generate power. (electric, diesel)

_____ 3. One of the first uses of airplanes was for delivery of _____. (people, mail)

_____ 4. There are _____ in every car for safety. (electric motors, seat belts)

_____ 5. Some cars now run on _____. (electricity, steam)

_____ 6. Gasoline used in cars comes from _____. (petroleum, rubber)

_____ 7. Gasoline has ingredients in it that reduce some _____. (pollution, accidents)

_____ 8. Materials used in cars must be strong but _____. (colorful, flexible)

Writing

Use complete sentences to answer question 9. (2 points)

9. What are some of the positive and negative characteristics of driving in the early days of cars versus modern cars and road conditions?

_____

_____

_____

_____

_____

_____

© Pearson Education, Inc.

Lesson 3: How have computers changed society?

Before You Read Lesson 3

Read each statement below. Place a check mark in the circle to indicate whether you agree or disagree with the statement.

	Agree	Disagree
1. Early computers were small and compact.	○	○
2. The World Wide Web has been around since the 1980s.	○	○
3. Computers can finish any task in a matter of seconds.	○	○
4. Computers can be used in telescopes, microscopes, and robots.	○	○

After You Read Lesson 3

Reread each statement above. If the lesson supports your choice, place a check mark in the *Correct* circle. Then explain how the text supports your choice. If the lesson does not support your choice, place a check mark in the *Incorrect* circle. Then explain why your choice is wrong.

	Correct	Incorrect
1. _____	○	○
2. _____	○	○
3. _____	○	○
4. _____	○	○

Notes for Home: Your child has completed a pre/post inventory of key concepts in the lesson.
Home Activity: Have your child write a paragraph about what life would be like without computers.

Name _____

Reviewing Terms: Matching

Match each definition with the correct term. Write the letter on the line next to the definition.

_____ 1. computer-based network of computers

_____ 2. a small piece of a computer that contains microscopic circuits

a. microchip

b. World Wide Web

Reviewing Concepts: True or False

Write **T** (True) or **F** (False) on the line before each statement.

_____ 3. Early computers replaced mechanical parts with electrical parts.

_____ 4. Microchips have caused the cost of computers to go down.

_____ 5. The World Wide Web was first developed for communication between physicists.

_____ 6. The spread of incorrect information and misinformation is not a problem for Web users.

_____ 7. Digital cameras use film to capture images and microchips to store them.

_____ 8. The invention of the computer has had little effect on other industries.

Applying Strategies: Summarize

Use complete sentences to answer question 9. (2 points)

9. Summarize the usefulness of computer-controlled tools.

_____

_____

_____

_____

Lesson 4: What technology is used in space?

Before You Read Lesson 4

Read each statement below. Place a check mark in the circle to indicate whether you agree or disagree with the statement.

	Agree	Disagree
1. Sputnik was the first satellite to orbit Earth.	○	○
2. The first person in space was Neil Armstrong.	○	○
3. A space station is used for very short periods of research.	○	○
4. The ISS allows people from different countries to research space activities.	○	○

After You Read Lesson 4

Reread each statement above. If the lesson supports your choice, place a check mark in the *Correct* circle. Then explain how the text supports your choice. If the lesson does not support your choice, place a check mark in the *Incorrect* circle. Then explain why your choice is wrong.

	Correct	Incorrect
1. _____	○	○
_____		
2. _____	○	○
_____		
3. _____	○	○
_____		
4. _____	○	○
_____		

Notes for Home: Your child has completed a pre/post inventory of key concepts in the lesson.
Home Activity: Ask your child to describe the International Space Station and to explain what it does.

Name _____

Lesson 4 Review

Use with page 588–591.

Reviewing Terms: Sentence Completion

Complete the sentence with the correct term.

_____ 1. A _____ is a place where people can live and work in space for long periods of time. (space agency, space station)

Reviewing Concepts: Sentence Completion

Complete each sentence with the correct word or phrase.

_____ 2. Strong political differences led to _____ between the United States and the Soviet Union in The Space Race. (cooperation, competition)

_____ 3. The first man in space was _____. (Armstrong, Gagarin)

_____ 4. The Space Shuttle is _____. (reusable, not reusable)

_____ 5. ISS stands for International _____ Station. (Satellite, Space)

_____ 6. The completed space station will have _____ solar array wings. (four, eight)

_____ 7. Rockets in the _____ Module keep the ISS in orbit. (Zarya Control, Zvezda Service)

_____ 8. Solar panels on the ISS turn _____ into electrical energy. (water, sunlight energy)

Applying Strategies: Calculating

9. The finished ISS will be about the length of a football field. A football field is 100 yards long. How many meters will the ISS be? (2 points)

© Pearson Education, Inc.

183A Lesson Review

Workbook

Map Scale and Topographic Maps

The map below uses a scale of 2 cm = 5 km. This means that a length of 2 cm on the map equals a distance of 5 km on Earth. Because 1 km = 1,000 m and 1 m = 100 cm, this scale is really a ratio of 2:500,000.

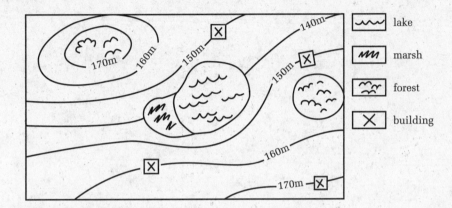

Use this topographic map of a state park to answer the questions.

1. If two buildings are 10 km apart, how far apart are they on the map?
   A. 2 cm
   B. 4 cm
   C. 6 cm
   D. 8 cm

2. If the two forests are 3 cm apart on the map, what is the actual distance between them?
   A. 2 km
   B. 5 km
   C. 7.5 km
   D. 10 km

3. Which of these features is found at an elevation of 140 m?
   A. Lake
   B. Forest
   C. Building
   D. All of the above

4. What is the highest elevation of a building?
   A. 150 m
   B. 160 m
   C. 170 m
   D. 180 m

Notes for Home: Your child learned how to read topographic maps.
Home Activity: Help your child find a topographic map of your area at the library or city hall. Find the elevations of your home and several local landmarks.

Notes

Dear Family,

Your child is learning how technology shapes our lives. In the chapter Technology in Our Lives, we learned how technology is used in our jobs and homes. We discovered how computers have created an information revolution. Finally, students learned about the history and future of space exploration.

Our class has learned many new vocabulary words that describe modern technology. Help your child to make these words a part of his or her own vocabulary by using them when you talk together about our modern world.

technology
inventor
manufacturing
assembly line
microchip
World Wide Web
space station

The following pages include activities that you and your child can do together. By participating in your child's education, you will help to bring the learning home.

Family Science Activity
Satellite Simulation

Materials:
- flashlight
- mirror

Steps

1 Explain that cell phones work via satellite. When a friend calls us, their telephone company's transmitter sends signals up to a satellite. These signals bounce off the satellite. Our telephone receives these signals and translates them into words.

2 Invite one other person to join you in this simulation. Stand a few feet away from each other. Position yourselves in the shape of a triangle. Give the "caller" a flashlight. Give the "satellite" a mirror.

3 Stand in a dark room. Have the "caller" shine the flashlight onto the "satellite." This simulates the sending of a signal. The "satellite" receives the signal from the "caller" by positioning the mirror so that the light shines onto it. Then, the "satellite" adjusts the mirror so that it shines on the "receiver." You have just sent a signal by satellite.

4 Discuss how long it took for you to send this beam of light from one location to another a few feet away. Then, ask your child how long it takes him or her to make a phone call via cell phone. Reiterate that our calls are sent and received very quickly via satellite.

Vocabulary Practice

Technology in Our Lives

Write the vocabulary word that completes each sentence. Use the numbered letters to complete the quotation.

1. Henry Ford developed the ___ ___ to speed up
   $\underline{\quad}_{10}$ $\underline{\quad}_{7}$ $\underline{\quad}_{2}$
   the production of cars.

2. An ___ is
   $\underline{\quad}_{5}$ $\underline{\quad}_{6}$
   someone who develops a new device or process.

3. The production of goods on a large scale is
   called ___.
   $\underline{\quad}_{3}$ $\underline{\quad}_{1}$

4. A ___
   $\underline{\quad}_{9}$
   is a small piece of a computer that contains
   $\underline{\quad}_{8}$ $\underline{\quad}_{4}$
   microscopic circuits.

A writer named Alvin Toffler wrote that "___ ___
$\underline{\quad}_{1}$ $\underline{\quad}_{2}$
makes more
$\underline{\quad}_{3}$ $\underline{\quad}_{4}$ $\underline{\quad}_{5}$ $\underline{\quad}_{6}$ $\underline{\quad}_{7}$ $\underline{\quad}_{8}$ $\underline{\quad}_{9}$ $\underline{\quad}_{10}$
technology possible."

ANSWERS: 1. assembly line; 2. inventor; 3. manufacturing; 4. microchip. PUZZLE ANSWER: technology.

Become an Inventor!

Invent an object that makes it easier for you to do something. Draw your invention below. Write sentences that tell about your invention.

How are invertebrates classified?

Scientists have named more than a million invertebrates. One way to identify an unknown organism is with a dichotomous key. A dichotomous key asks a series of questions about an organism. Follow the arrows to find out about the unknown organism.

Dichotomous Key

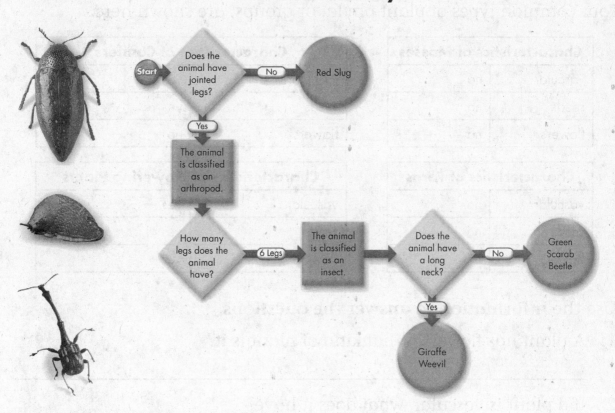

Answer these questions about the pictures above.

1. Are the organisms vertebrates or invertebrates?

   _____

2. How is the red slug different from the other organisms?

   _____

3. What are organisms with six jointed legs called?

   _____

4. How is the giraffe weevil like the green scarab beetle?

   _____

What are the qualities of some plants?

All plants use sunlight, water, and carbon dioxide to make their own sugar for food. Many plants are vascular. This means the plant has special tubes for carrying food and water to all its parts. Organisms in the plant kingdom are grouped according to shared characteristics. Four common types of plant phyla, or groups, are shown here.

Characteristics of Mosses	
vascular	no
seeds	no
flowers	no

Characteristics of Conifers	
vascular	yes
seeds	yes
flowers	no

Characteristics of Ferns	
vascular	no
seeds	no
flowers	no

Characteristics of Flowering Plants	
vascular	yes
seeds	yes
flowers	yes

Use the information to answer the questions.

1. A plant has flowers. What kind of plant is it?

    _____

2. If a plant is vascular, what does it have?

    _____

3. How are ferns like mosses?

    _____

4. How are conifers like flowering plants?

    _____

5. A plant is vascular and has no flowers. What do you need to know before you can classify it?

    _____

    _____

Name _____

What are the parts of an animal cell?

Cells are the smallest living parts of a plant or animal. Each part of a cell has a special job. The cell shown below is an animal cell.

Parts of an Animal Cell

Nucleus: Almost every nucleus in your body has 46 chromosomes. Each chromosome has hundreds of genes.

Cell membrane: The cell membrane can be compared to your skin. They are both outside surfaces.

Vacuole: Vacuoles store and break down material.

Cytoplasm: Cytoplasm is all the material of the cell between the cell membrane and the nucleus.

Mitochondria: Mitochondria are the cell's power producers. They take in oxygen and food and combine them to produce energy.

Answer these questions about the picture above.

1. How many parts does an animal cell have?

   _____

2. Which part is at the center of the cell?

   _____

3. How is the cell membrane like your skin?

   _____

4. Which part makes up most of the cell?

   _____

5. Which parts of the cell create energy?

   _____

What are the tissues of the skin?

Skin protects your insides, keeps out germs, and prevents too much water from leaving the body. Your skin has many layers and tissues that work together. Nerve cells help you sense touch and temperature. Blood vessels carry food and oxygen to cells. Oil glands make oil to keep skin soft.

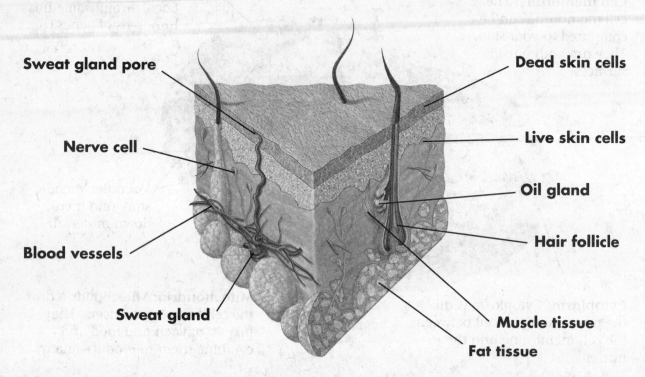

Sweat gland pore

Nerve cell

Blood vessels

Sweat gland

Dead skin cells

Live skin cells

Oil gland

Hair follicle

Muscle tissue

Fat tissue

Use the diagram and information to answer each question.

1. What is the top layer of skin made of?

_____

2. What do blood vessels in skin tissue do?

_____

3. What helps you feel if water from the tap is hot or cold?

_____

4. What is under muscle tissue?

_____

5. What helps to keep your skin soft?

_____

What is your respiratory system?

Your respiratory system is at work when you smell, talk, walk, and breathe. The job of your respiratory system is to carry gases between the outside air and your blood. Your respiratory system allows oxygen to enter the blood. It also allows carbon dioxide to leave the blood.

The Respiratory System

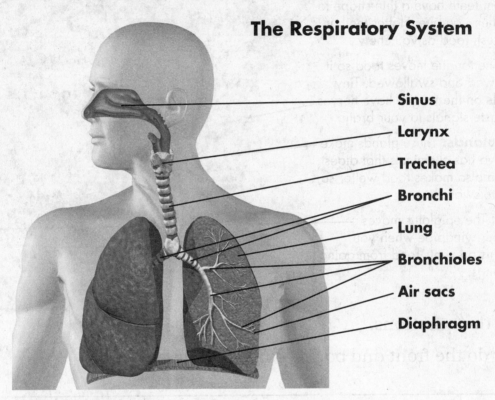

- Sinus
- Larynx
- Trachea
- Bronchi
- Lung
- Bronchioles
- Air sacs
- Diaphragm

Answer these questions.

1. Which tube carries air from the larynx to the bronchi?

   _____

2. Which parts of your respiratory system are inside the lungs?

   _____

3. Name the muscle below your lungs that helps you breathe.

   _____

4. What is the job of your respiratory system?

   _____

5. When is your respiratory system at work?

   _____

Name _____

What is the mouth?

Your body has to digest food before your cells can use it. The digestive system is made up of many organs that work together. Chewing is the first step of digestion.

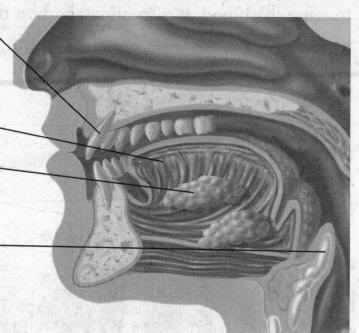

Teeth: Front teeth have a thin shape to cut food when you bite. Flatter teeth in the back crush food as you chew.

Tongue: The tongue moves food so it can be chewed and swallowed. Tiny **taste buds** on the tongue have nerves that send taste signals to your brain.

Salivary glands: These glands make saliva. Saliva has chemicals that digest food. Saliva also makes food wetter so it is easier to swallow.

Epiglottis: The epiglottis moves to cover your windpipe when you swallow. This prevents food from going into your lungs.

Answer the questions.

1. How do the front and back teeth look different?

   _____

2. Where are taste buds located?

   _____

3. What do the chemicals in saliva do?

   _____

4. What covers your windpipe when you swallow?

   _____

5. How does having different shaped teeth in front and back help you eat?

   _____

6. How does saliva make food easier to swallow?

   _____

Name _____

What are the layers of a leaf?

Leaves are organs made of cells and tissues. The diagram below shows a cross-section of a leaf. The epidermis tissue is like your skin. It protects the plant. The spongy tissue has spaces that air can pass through. Leaf openings at the bottom of the leaf let air in and out of the spongy tissue. The vessel tissue carries food and water throughout the plant.

Leaf Tissues

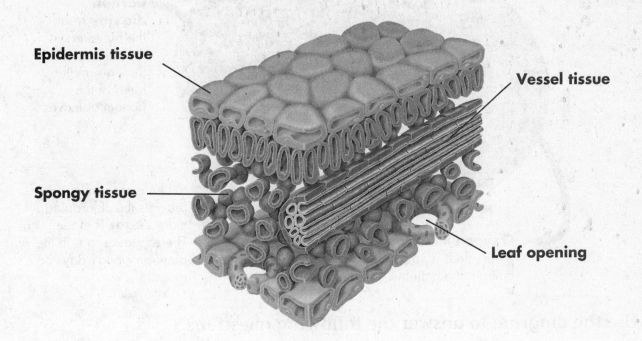

Epidermis tissue

Vessel tissue

Spongy tissue

Leaf opening

Answer these questions about the picture above.

1. How many tissues does a leaf have?

_____

2. Which tissue helps protect the plant?

_____

3. What lets air in and out of the spongy tissue?

_____

4. Which tissue carries food and water throughout the plant?

_____

What is photosynthesis?

Photosynthesis is the process that plants use to make sugar for food. Photosynthesis happens in the chloroplasts of plant cells.

Chloroplast
Inside a chloroplast are structures that look like stacked plates. They contain chlorophyll.

Chlorophyll absorbs sunlight. This gives the cell energy to make sugar from carbon dioxide and water.

Water enters the chloroplast.

Carbon dioxide from the air enters the chloroplast through small holes in the bottom of leaves.

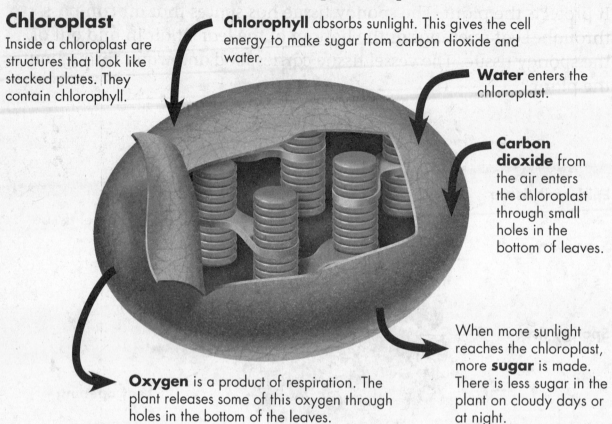

Oxygen is a product of respiration. The plant releases some of this oxygen through holes in the bottom of the leaves.

When more sunlight reaches the chloroplast, more **sugar** is made. There is less sugar in the plant on cloudy days or at night.

Use the diagram to answer the following questions.

1. What does the chloroplast absorb?

_____

2. What does the chloroplast release?

_____

3. What gives a plant energy to make sugar?

_____

4. What does chlorophyll do?

_____

5. How does light affect how much sugar a plant makes?

_____

How does energy move through a food web?

All organisms need energy to live. Organisms get energy by eating food. Energy passes through an ecosystem. Producers are organisms that make their own food. Consumers are organisms that get energy by eating other organisms.

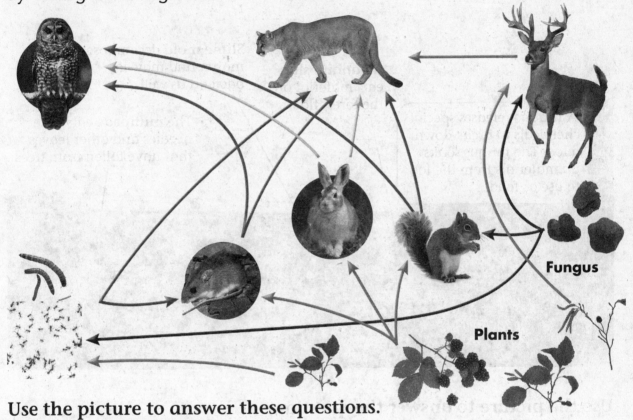

Fungus

Plants

Use the picture to answer these questions.

1. What does the squirrel eat for energy?

   _____

2. Which animal eats both plants and animals?

   _____

3. How does energy pass from plants to the spotted owl?

   _____

   _____

4. What are the producers in the food web?

   _____

Name _____

How are minerals and nutrients recycled?

Decomposers eat waste and dead matter. They break material into smaller pieces and put it back into the soil. Living organisms can then use the minerals and nutrients from waste. Decomposers help recycle minerals and nutrients.

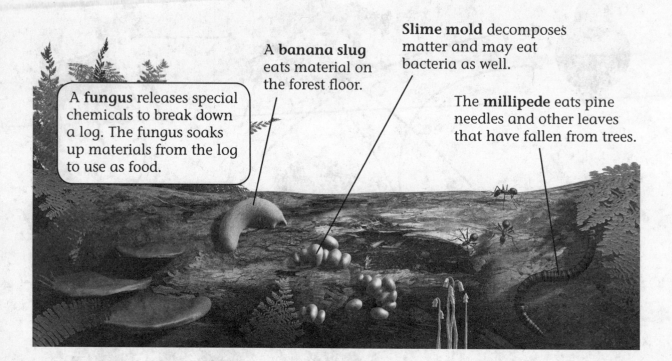

A **fungus** releases special chemicals to break down a log. The fungus soaks up materials from the log to use as food.

A **banana slug** eats material on the forest floor.

Slime mold decomposes matter and may eat bacteria as well.

The **millipede** eats pine needles and other leaves that have fallen from trees.

Use the picture to answer the questions.

1. How does a fungus break down a log?

_____

2. Which decomposer may also eat bacteria?

_____

3. How are the banana slug and millipede alike?

_____

4. How do decomposers help recycle minerals and nutrients?

_____

_____

How do ecosystems change?

Both animals and people can change ecosystems.

A Beaver Dam Beavers build a dam to make a new pond where they can be safe from predators.

Acid Rain Damage Acid rain is rain that has absorbed certain kinds of air pollution. It damages forests, soils, and lakes.

A Landfill Most garbage ends up in landfills. Landfills may cover a few acres or a few thousand acres. They are eventually covered with soil and grass.

Answer these questions about the pictures above.

1. Which photo or photos show a change caused by animals?

   _____

2. Which photos show changes caused by people?

   _____

3. What is acid rain?

   _____

4. What has acid rain done to the forest?

   _____

5. Why do you think landfills are eventually covered with soil and grass?

   _____

What are two kinds of ways animals are adapted?

Organisms adapt to fit their environments. Some adaptations are structural. They are changed body parts that help an organism survive. Other adaptations are behavioral. They are activities that help organisms. Both structural and behavioral adaptations are inherited.

The hummingbird has legs that can tuck close to the body. This makes it easier for the hummingbird to fly. This is a structural adaptation.

The hummingbird is born knowing how to make a nest. It is also born knowing how to take care of its offspring. These are behavioral adaptations.

Answer these questions.

1. What structural adaptation makes it easier for a hummingbird to fly?

   _____

2. What is the bird doing in the picture? Is this a structural or behavioral adaptation?

   _____

3. What are two behavioral adaptations the little birds have inherited?

   _____

4. How are physical and behavioral adaptations helpful to animals?

   _____

How do ocean currents affect ocean temperature?

The temperature of ocean water varies. Water near the poles is colder than water near the Equator. However, some currents carry warm water toward the poles. The Gulf Stream Current moves warm water from the Caribbean Sea to the North Atlantic Ocean. Other currents, such as the California Current, carries cold water toward the Equator.

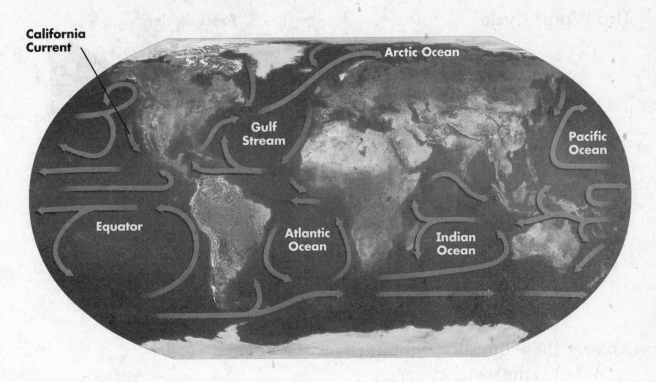

Answer these questions about ocean currents.

1. How is the water temperature near the poles different from near the Equator?

   _____

2. Which current carries warm water to the poles?

   _____

3. Which current flows southward along the coast of the United States?

   _____

Name _____

What is the water cycle?

The water cycle is the repeated movement of water through the environment. There are four steps in the water cycle. Evaporation is the changing of liquid water to water vapor. In condensation, the water vapor turns into water droplets. These droplets make up clouds. In precipitation, water can fall from clouds as rain, snow, sleet, or hail. Runoff occurs when this water moves downhill.

The Water Cycle

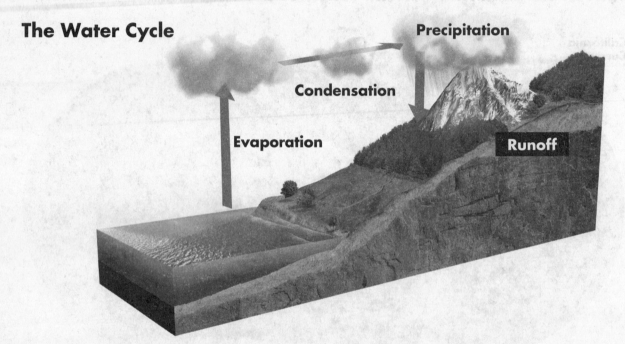

Precipitation

Condensation

Evaporation

Runoff

Answer these questions about the water cycle.

1. What is the water cycle?

    _____

2. In which step does water vapor turn into water droplets?

    _____

3. What are four forms of precipitation?

    _____

4. When does runoff occur?

    _____

5. In which step does liquid water to change to water vapor?

    _____

Name _____

Use with Chapter 8, pp. 234–235

What are air masses?

Large bodies of air drift across the globe. There are four basic kinds of air masses. The weather is mostly caused by the type of air mass in the area at the moment. Weather changes when air masses are pushed together.

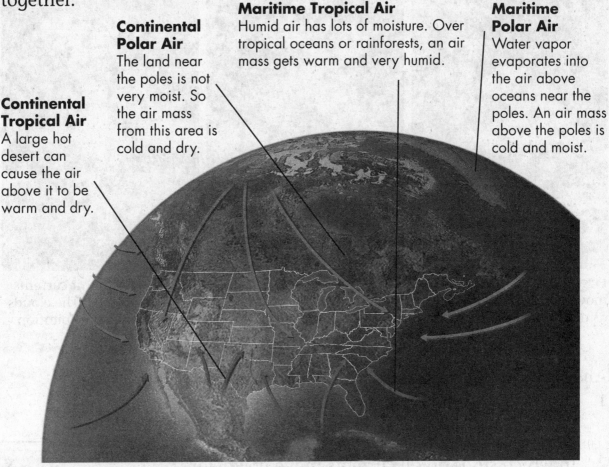

Continental Polar Air
The land near the poles is not very moist. So the air mass from this area is cold and dry.

Maritime Tropical Air
Humid air has lots of moisture. Over tropical oceans or rainforests, an air mass gets warm and very humid.

Maritime Polar Air
Water vapor evaporates into the air above oceans near the poles. An air mass above the poles is cold and moist.

Continental Tropical Air
A large hot desert can cause the air above it to be warm and dry.

Answer these questions.

1. What kind of air mass forms at Earth's poles?

_____

2. What kind of air mass is warm and very humid?

_____

3. What kind of air mass is likely to form over a desert?

_____

4. What kind of air mass would you expect over northern Canada?

_____

Name _____

What causes severe weather?

Thunderstorms can form in different ways. These are the stages of a thunderstorm.

First stage: All air currents move upward. Clouds grow as moisture condenses.

Second stage: Air currents are mixed. Precipitation falls. This pulls some air down.

Final stage: All air currents move downward. The clouds get smaller as precipitation leaves.

Answer these questions about the pictures above.

1. In which stage(s) does precipitation fall?

_____

2. In which stage do all currents move downward?

_____

3. In which stage are air currents mixed?

_____

4. In which stage do clouds grow? Why do they grow?

_____

5. In which stage do clouds get smaller? Why do they get smaller?

_____

What are the mantle and the core?

Earth has four layers: the crust, the mantle, the outer core, and the inner core. The mantle has convection currents. These currents make cooler rock flow down and hotter rock flow up. These currents also push and pull on Earth's plates. This is one cause of earthquakes. The core is at the center of Earth. The outer core is liquid. The inner core is very hot iron. The currents in the core make Earth's magnetic field.

Layer	Average Thickness
crust	31 km
mantle	2900 km
outer core	2221 km
inner core	1255 km radius

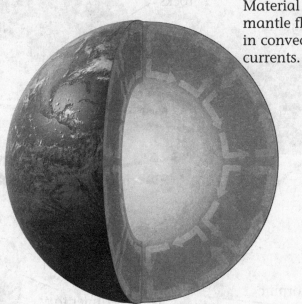

Material in the mantle flows in convection currents.

Answer these questions about the chart above.

1. Which of Earth's layers is the thinnest?

_____

2. Which of Earth's layers is the thickest?

_____

Write the answers to the questions on the lines.

3. How do convection currents in the mantle cause earthquakes?

_____

4. Which layer is at the center of Earth?

_____

5. What causes Earth's magnetic field?

_____

What is the rock cycle?

Rocks on Earth are constantly destroyed and formed. There are three forms of rock: igneous, metamorphic, and sedimentary. Rocks can change from one form to another in any order. Some changes happen very quickly. Other changes can take millions of years. Some rocks stay the same for millions of years.

The Rock Cycle

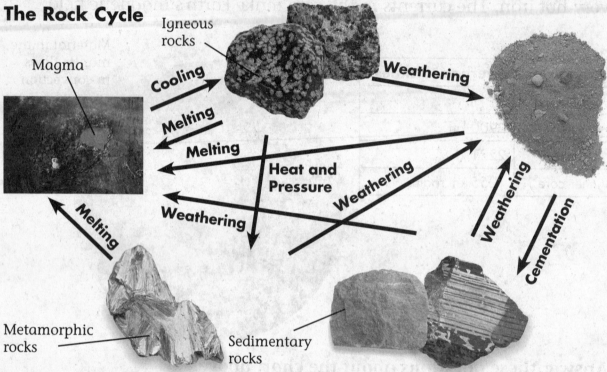

Magma

Igneous rocks

Cooling

Melting

Melting

Heat and Pressure

Weathering

Weathering

Weathering

Weathering

Cementation

Melting

Weathering

Metamorphic rocks

Sedimentary rocks

Answer these questions.

1. Describe how igneous rock can change to metamorphic rock.

_____

2. Describe two processes that can change metamorphic rock.

_____

3. Which steps in the rock cycle are caused by temperature?

_____

4. What change is caused by cementation?

_____

5. How long does can it take for a rock to change to another form?

_____

What are nonrenewable and renewable energy resources?

Renewable resources can be replaced. Nonrenewable resources cannot be replaced.

These wind turbines use energy from the wind to make electricity.

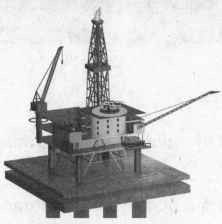

Oil drills make deep holes in Earth to reach oil. The oil is either on land or beneath the ocean floor.

The water wheel uses the energy of flowing water to power saws, looms, or other machines.

Fill in the blanks and answer these questions.

1. A _____ resource cannot be replaced.

2. A _____ resource can be replaced.

3. Which nonrenewable resource is being collected?

   _____

4. Which two renewable resources are being collected?

   _____

5. Which of these resources can be collected on land or beneath the

   ocean floor? _____

© Pearson Education, Inc.

Workbook

Name _____

How can air, water, and soil be damaged?

Air, soil, and water are important resources. Changes in the environment can damage these resources. These changes can lead to health problems for humans and other organisms. They can also damage buildings and other structures.

Gasses given off by a car

Trash on soil

Oil spill

Answer these questions.

1. Which photo shows one way that air quality can be damaged?

   _____

2. Which photo shows one way that soil quality can be damaged?

   _____

3. What might damage to the environment lead to?

   _____

4. Why are water, air, and soil important resources?

   _____

5. Describe another way that water can be damaged.

   _____

What are atoms?

An atom is the smallest particle of an element. An atom's center is called the nucleus. It usually has neutrons and protons. A neutron has no electrical charge. A proton has a positive charge. An atom is identified by the number of protons it has. Electrons move around protons and neutrons. An electron has a negative charge. Electrons may join or leave atoms, or be shared by atoms.

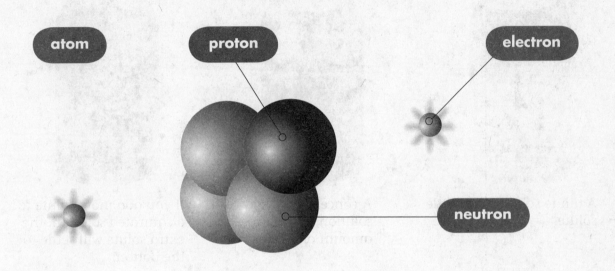

atom   **proton**   **electron**   **neutron**

Answer these questions about atoms.

1. What is the smallest particle of an element called?

    _____

2. Which part of an atom has neutrons and protons?

    _____

3. How is an atom identified?

    _____

4. What moves around protons and neutrons?

    _____

5. What kind of electrical charge does a neutron have?

    _____

Name _____

What are mixtures and solutions?

A solution is a special kind of mixture. For example, sugar and water make a mixture called a solution. In this solution, the solute is sugar. Solutions with little solute are called **dilute**. Solutions with a lot of solute are **concentrated**.

A dilute solution has little solute.

A concentrated solution has a large amount of solute.

If you add more solute to a saturated solution, the extra solute will settle to the bottom.

Answer these questions.

1. How can you recognize the solute in these pictures?

   _____

2. Which solution is dilute? Does it have a little or a lot of solute?

   _____

3. Which solution is concentrated? Does it have a little or a lot of solute?

   _____

4. In a sugar and water solution, what is the solute?

   _____

5. What happens if you add more solute to a saturated solution?

   _____

What are chemical changes?

When a chemical change happens, atoms rearrange themselves so that one kind of matter changes into a completely different kind of matter. Some chemical changes are easy to see. Other chemical changes are hard to see.

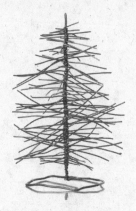

Copper wire tree

Copper tree in chemical solution

Later: Solid crystals form.

Answer these questions.

1. What happens in a chemical change?

   _____

2. Does this experiment show a physical change or a chemical change? How do you know?

   _____

3. Do you think the results would be the same if you used water instead of chemical solution? Explain.

   _____

   _____

4. What do you notice about the top of the wire tree?

   _____

5. What is the difference between a physical change and a chemical change?

   _____

What are some kinds of chemical reactions?

This chart shows three important kinds of chemical reactions. Look at the model for each kind of reaction.

reaction	model
decomposition	○● ➡ ○+●
combination	○+● ➡ ○●
replacement	●○+●○ ➡ ●● +○○

- In a **decomposition** reaction, compounds split apart to form smaller compounds.
- In a **combination** reaction, elements or compounds come together to form new compounds.
- In a **replacement** reaction, one or more compounds split apart and the parts switch places.

Answer these questions using the chart above.

1. How does the model show what happens in a decomposition reaction?

   _____

2. Rust happens when iron and sulfur come together to form iron sulfide. Which model shows this type of chemical reaction? Why?

   _____

   _____

3. When wax in a candle burns, molecules of carbon and hydrogen and molecules of oxygen break apart. They rejoin in new compounds such as carbon dioxide and water. What kind of chemical reaction is this? Why?

   _____

   _____

What does friction do?

Friction is the force that results when two materials rub against each other. Friction slows down the motion of an object or keeps it from starting to move.

A bicycle has many features that increase friction.

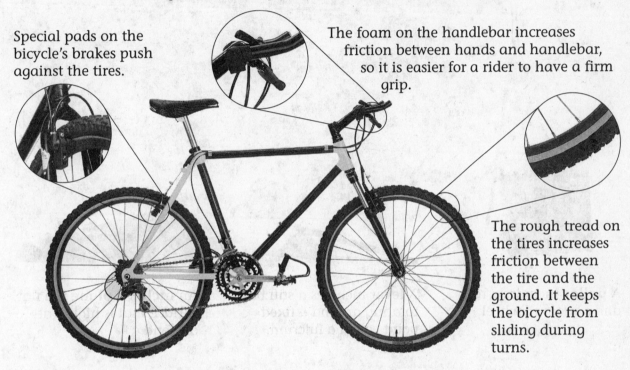

Special pads on the bicycle's brakes push against the tires.

The foam on the handlebar increases friction between hands and handlebar, so it is easier for a rider to have a firm grip.

The rough tread on the tires increases friction between the tire and the ground. It keeps the bicycle from sliding during turns.

Answer these questions about friction.

1. What two materials rub together to help slow or stop the bicycle?

   _____

2. What two materials help a rider keep a firm grip on the handlebar?

   _____

3. What keeps the bicycle from sliding during turns?

   _____

4. What would happen if the brake pads wore out?

   _____

5. What do you have to do to make sure your bike is safe to ride?

Name _____

What are some simple machines?

Machines make work easier. They do not reduce the amount of work to be done. Simple machines are machines with only a few parts, such as pulleys, levers, and inclined planes.

A **pulley** includes a rope and a grooved wheel.

A **lever** includes a stiff bar rotating around a fixed point called a fulcrum.

An **inclined plane** is a flat surface that is higher at one end.

Answer these questions about simple machines.

1. How do machines help us?

_____

2. What is a simple machine?

_____

3. What are three examples of simple machines?

_____

4. Which simple machine has a flat surface that is higher at one end?

_____

5. What is a pulley made of?

_____

© Pearson Education, Inc.

What is light energy?

Light is a part of the electromagnetic spectrum. Light travels in waves that have many frequencies and wavelengths. The diagram below shows the electromagnetic spectrum. The shortest wavelengths are at the far left. The longest wavelengths are at the far right.

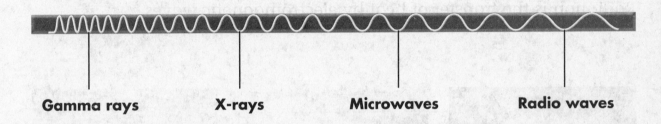

Gamma rays   **X-rays**   **Microwaves**   **Radio waves**

Answer these questions about light energy.

1. How does light travel?

    _____

2. How do the waves of the electromagnetic spectrum differ?

    _____

3. What are the longest wavelengths in the electromagnetic spectrum?

    _____

4. Are gamma rays shorter or longer than X-rays?

    _____

5. Are radio waves shorter or longer than X-rays?

© Pearson Education, Inc.

What are conduction, convection, and radiation?

Thermal energy naturally flows between substances of different temperatures. The flow of thermal energy is heat. Heat moves in three ways. Conduction is the transfer of heat between objects that are in contact. Convection is the transfer of heat by a moving liquid or gas. Radiation is the transfer of heat by electromagnetic waves.

Conduction A volcano's lava heats the water it touches.

Currents of warmed water carry heat through the tank by **convection**.

Radiation from the Sun warms this greenhouse.

Answer these questions.

1. How does thermal energy flow?

   _____

2. What word is used to describe the flow of thermal energy?

   _____

3. Does a light bulb heat the air around it by conduction, convection, or radiation?

   _____

4. How does a pan on a stove get hot?

   _____

5. How does warm water in the ocean carry heat?

   _____

Name _____

What is current?

A wire can carry an electric current. Most wires are made of a metal that is a good conductor, such as copper. The metal is surrounded by plastic or rubber insulation to make the wire safe to touch. Electrons are particles of an atom. When a power source is turned on, the electrons flow through the wire in the same direction.

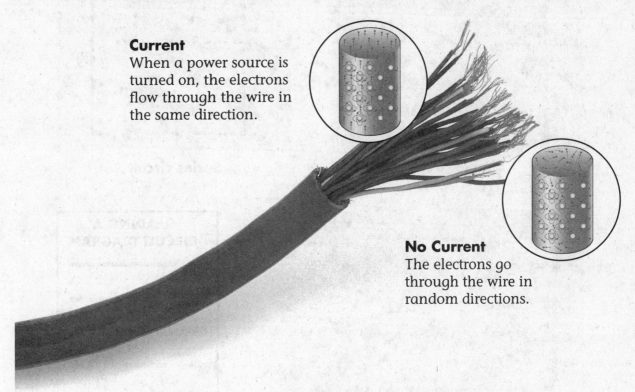

Current
When a power source is turned on, the electrons flow through the wire in the same direction.

No Current
The electrons go through the wire in random directions.

Answer these questions about the pictures above.

1. Which diagram shows the wire that is not plugged in?

    _____

2. Describe the movements of the electrons in a wire that is not plugged in?

    _____

3. How do charged electrons change when a power source is turned on?

    _____

4. Why are wires covered with plastic or rubber insulation?

    _____

© Pearson Education, Inc.

What is a circuit diagram?

A circuit diagram is a map of an electric circuit. Symbols on a circuit diagram stand for each part of the circuit.

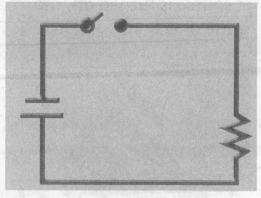

Simple circuit

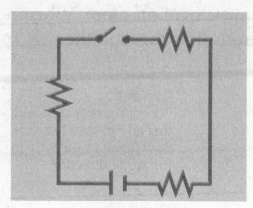

Series circuit

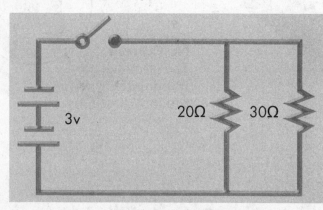

Complex circuit

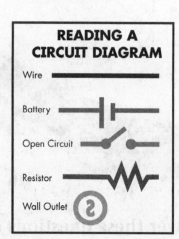

Answer these questions about the pictures above.

1. Which of these circuit diagrams contains three resistors?

   _____

2. Which of these circuit diagrams shows a parallel circuit?

   _____

3. How can you tell if a circuit is open?

   _____

4. What is the power source for each of these circuits?

   _____

What are constellations?

By "connecting the dots" formed by the stars, people see patterns in the night sky. There are 88 recognized constellations. A constellation is an area of the sky and all the stars in that area. The stars appear to move or change position because of Earth's rotation.

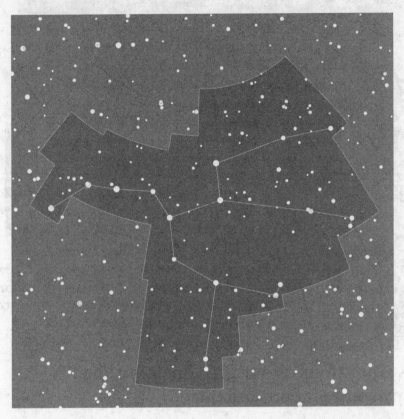

Answer these questions about the picture above.

1. Estimate how many stars are visible in this part of the sky.

   _____

2. Suppose you see this pattern of stars at midnight. Will the sky look different two hours later?

   _____

3. Choose one star and try to describe its location so that another student will know exactly which star you chose.

   _____

4. Why do the stars appear to move during the night?

   _____

What are some constellations?

Ursa Major Ursa is the Latin word for *bear*.
The Big Dipper forms the bear's back and tail.

Centaurus The centaur was a character in Greek mythology that was half human and half horse.

Scorpius looks like a scorpion.

Answer these questions about the constellations.

1. How many constellations are there?

_____

2. Does a constellation include **only** the stars connected by the imaginary lines that create a shape?

_____

3. What was the constellation Centaurus named after?

_____

_____

4. How does dividing the sky into constellations make studying the stars easier?

_____

_____

What causes the seasons?

The tilt of Earth causes parts of Earth to receive different amounts of sunlight throughout the year. The amount of sunlight an area receives creates its seasons. This also causes the number of daylight hours to change during the year. The picture below shows the Northern Hemisphere's seasons.

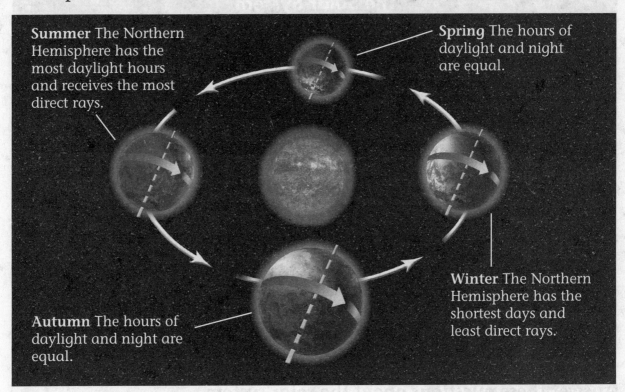

Summer The Northern Hemisphere has the most daylight hours and receives the most direct rays.

Spring The hours of daylight and night are equal.

Autumn The hours of daylight and night are equal.

Winter The Northern Hemisphere has the shortest days and least direct rays.

Answer these questions.

1. During which seasons are the hours of daylight and night equal?

   _____

2. What creates the seasons?

   _____

3. During which season does the Northern Hemisphere receive the least amount of sunlight?

   _____

4. What causes parts of Earth to receive different amounts of sunlight throughout the year?

   _____

© Pearson Education, Inc.

Name _____

What are the parts of the solar system?

The solar system includes the Sun and its nine planets, as well as many moons, asteroids, and comets.

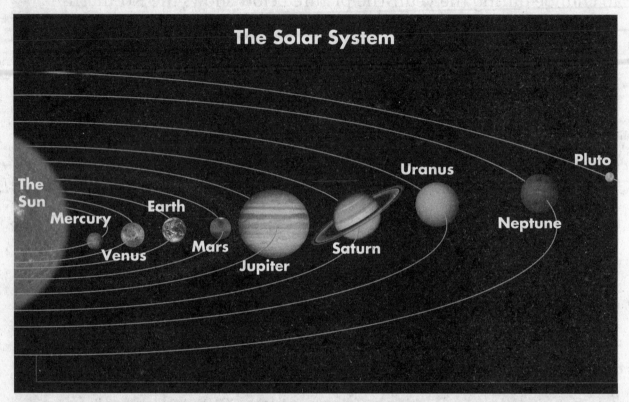

The Solar System

Answer these questions about the solar system.

1. Does Mercury travel faster in its orbit than Neptune? Why?

_____

2. Which planets are closer to the Sun than Earth?

_____

3. What is the largest body in the solar system?

_____

4. Which planet is farthest from the Sun?

_____

5. Which planet is the largest in diameter?

_____

© Pearson Education, Inc.

Workbook

Name _____

What is an assembly line?

In an assembly line, a product moves through the factory while workers add parts to it. We use the assembly line to make many products in less time.

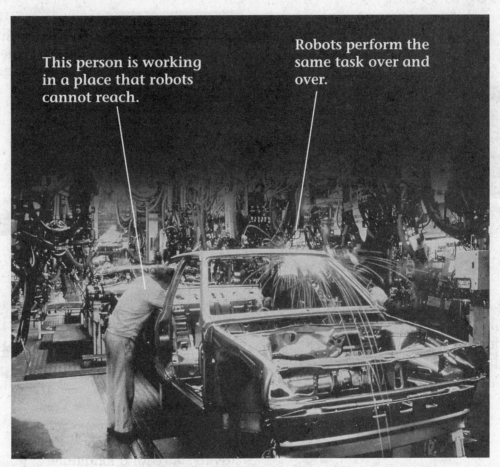

This person is working in a place that robots cannot reach.

Robots perform the same task over and over.

Answer these questions about the assembly line above.

1. What is being built on the assembly line?

   _____

2. Who is working on the assembly line?

   _____

3. What happens to a product as it moves through the factory?

   _____

4. Why do we use the assembly line?

   _____

© Pearson Education, Inc.

Name _____

What is the history of space exploration?

This timeline shows some important events in the exploration of space from 1957 to 1986.

1957: Sputnik 1 is the first satellite to orbit Earth.

1981: The Space Shuttle is the first reusable spaceship.

| 1950 | 1960 | 1970 | 1980 | 1990 |

1969: Neil Armstrong and Buzz Aldrin are the first people to walk on the Moon.

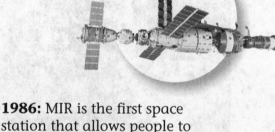

1986: MIR is the first space station that allows people to stay in space for a long time.

Answer these questions about the pictures above.

1. What was Sputnik 1?

_____

2. What was invented in 1981?

_____

3. Who walked on the Moon first?

_____

4. What was the MIR?

_____

Picture Credits

Illustration

189, 190, 191, 192 Leonello Calvetti
193, 194 Jeff Mangiat
196, 203 Adam Benton
204 Tony Randazzo
219 Bob Kayganich

Photographs

Every effort has been made to secure permission and provide appropriate credit for photographic material. The publisher deeply regrets any omission and pledges to correct errors called to its attention in subsequent editions.

Unless otherwise acknowledged, all photographs are the property of Scott Foresman, a division of Pearson Education.

187 © DK Images, © Tony Wharton; Frank Lane Picture Agency/Corbis. 195 © Michael Sewell/Peter Arnold, Inc., © DK Images, © Daniel Cox/Getty Images, © Michael Quinton/ Minden Pictures, © John Shaw/Tom Stack & Associates, Inc., Getty Images. 197 © Pat O'Hara/Corbis, © Ted Spiegel/Corbis, Corbis. 198 © Michael & Patricia Fogden/Minden Pictures. 204 © DK Images, Natural History Museum/© DK Images. 205 © /Corbis. 206 © Pat J. Groves, Ecoscene/Corbis, © Roger Ressmeyer/Corbis, AP/Wide World Photos. 208 © DK Images. 209 © DK Images. 211 © DK Images. 215 © DK Images. 218 © DK Images. 220 Getty Images, © JPL/NASA, Getty Images, Corbis, © JPL/NASA, © Comstock Inc., © NASA/Roger Ressmeyer/Corbis, NASA. 221 © Luis Castaneda Inc./Getty Images. 222 © Hulton Collection/Getty Images

Notes

Notes

Notes

Notes

Notes

Notes

Notes